Wissenschaftliche Abhandlungen
Band LXII/2

Musicological Studies
Vol. LXII/2

Claremont Cultural Studies

THE MEDIEVAL WEST MEETS
THE REST OF THE WORLD

general editor

Nancy van Deusen

The Institute of Mediaeval Music
Ottawa, Canada

The Institute of Mediaeval Music
1270 Lampman Crescent
Ottawa, Canada
K2C 1P8

ISBN 0-931902-94-0

THE MEDIEVAL WEST MEETS THE REST OF THE WORLD

CONTENTS

A Preface

The Medieval West Meets the Rest of the World

One of the most important reasons to travel is that one acquires another, in some ways quite different, personality. Reaction to, interaction with, reflection upon another, unaccustomed, less consciously-accepted environment produce significant changes, while perhaps reinforcing basic, essential strengths.

The analogy—not to be accepted in its entirety, because it is too simplistic—applies to the situation at hand, namely, medieval concepts on the move, so to speak, confronting and interacting with other geographical and temporal cultures. We have all consciously tried not to look for causes and effects; rather, in dealing with what we considered to be an interesting, even outstanding element noticed in the culture of our own expertise, endeavored to sensitively observe the directions in which that particular aspect itself led us. The results—as varied and diverse as they are—mirror the variety and marvellous diversity of the lives, peoples, entire civilizations of this planet.

This project surely would have interested the distinguished, provocative, and influential scholar in whose memory the conference which formed the occasion for the interaction documented by this volume was held, Professor Lynn White, Jr. Former president of Mills College, founder of the Center for Medieval and Renaissance Studies, University of California, Los Angeles, conceptual leader in an emerging field of the study of medieval technology, Lynn White was very much "at home" in California, creating a capacious intellectual environment where he was, yet reaching out—an intellectual explorer to the end of his life—observing the "resonances" of medieval concepts with other world cultures.

Accordingly, interactions between places and times form the structure of this volume: there are resonances in thought, mathematics, musical intervals and classifications, and stories. Papers include parallels to concepts of the "End of the Middle Ages," and the European Reformation in other world religious civilizations (Crerar Douglas), interactions between ritual and ordinary, everyday, culture in a Swiss-German *computus* (Barnabas Hughes), relationships between Arabic, Greek, Latin, and Jewish mental cultures in the early Aristotelian reception within a Latin intellectual environment (James Otte), with a conclusion by Kees Bolle that cultural interaction forms "stimulus for our locked-up specializations to bring to the attention of the entire university the force and relevance of our documents." James Porter eloquently summarizes the structural and conceptual connections between world music civilizations in his introduction to the contributions of musicologists Doris Stockmann, José Maceda, and Nancy van Deusen; and Scott Littleton, with Linda Peterson Malcor bring to the attention ways in which people—and ideas—arrive from astonishing destinations. Single conceptual components are preserved intact, as they travel from one place—or time—to another.

The conference, *East Meets West: The Resonance of Medieval European Concepts with the Rest of the World,* was held to honor the memory of Lynn White, Jr., February 9–10, 1990, at California State University, Northridge. The support of this university as well as the editorial and production assistance of Wendy Pronin, Carey Reid, and, especially, Nancy Bowen are gratefully acknowledged.

NANCY VAN DEUSEN
The Claremont Graduate School
November, 1994

Yin and *Yang* as Insignia of the Armigeri: Chinese Cosmological Symbols on Late Roman Shields

by Gunar Freibergs

Among the handful of illuminated manuscripts whose contents have been transmitted from late antiquity is a richly adorned administrative document known as the *Notitia dignitatum*.[1] Prepared between the years A.D. 395 and 430, apparently on the initiative of some anonymous official(s) in the imperial notarial offices, it is a detailed register of the civil and military dignitaries in the late Roman Empire.[2] A feature which makes the *Notitia* an object of particular significance to students of the art of the Late Empire is the fact that in addition to listing the administrators who staffed the imperial bureaucracy, it also furnishes illustrations of their official accoutrements and insignia. Among the most interesting of these are images of some 265

Acknowledgments: Earlier versions of this article were read at the annual conference of the Southern California Academy of Sciences, Los Angeles, on May 11, 1984, and at "The Medieval West Meets the Rest of the World: Medieval Concepts and Their Resonance," a symposium in honor of Lynn White, Jr., California State University, Northridge, on February 10, 1990. I wish to thank the late Lynn White, Jr. and Richard Rudolph, both of the University of California at Los Angeles, Helmut Nickel, formerly curator of arms and armor at the Metropolitan Museum of Art in New York, Robert Grigg of the University of California at Davis, James K. Otte of the University of San Diego, and Sharie Meyer for furnishing me with a variety of helpful source and reference materials, John E. Wills, Jr., Richard C. Dales, D. Brendan Nagle and Paul W. Knoll, all of the University of Southern California, for lending advice and encouragement, and Mary F. Romig and C. Scott Littleton for their readiness to critique a draft of this manuscript. They should not, however, be held responsible for the conclusions drawn in this paper, which are my own.

[1] The full title is *Notitia dignitatum omnium, tam civilium quam militarium.* The text and illustrations survive in three fifteenth- and sixteenth-century copies of a tenth-century copy (the now lost *Codex Spirensis*) of the late Roman original. The critical edition was published by Otto Seeck, *Notitia Dignitatum* (Frankfurt, 1876). For details concerning the manuscript tradition and the transmission of the text and illustrations, see J. J. G. Alexander, "The Illustrated Manuscripts of the Notitia Dignitatum," *Aspects of the Notitia Dignitatum,* ed. R. Goodburn and P. Bartholomew, B.A.R. Supplementary Series 15 (Oxford, 1976), 11–25; Robert J. Grigg, "Portrait-Bearing Codicils in the Illustrations of the Notitia Dignitatum?" *Journal of Roman Studies* 69 (1979), 107–124.

[2] Pamela C. Berger, *The Insignia of the Notitia Dignitatum* (New York, 1981), pp. xxi–xxv, 1–23; J. C. Mann, "What Was the Notitia Dignitatum For?" *Aspects of the Notitia Dignitatum,* pp. 1–9. Studies on the civil and military administrative organization as revealed by the *Notitia* can be found in Dietrich Hoffmann, *Das spätrömische Bewegungsheer und die Notitia dignitatum,* 2 vols. (Düsseldorf, 1969–70) and A. H. M. Jones, *The Later Roman Empire, 284–602,* 2 vols. (Norman, Okla., 1964), 2:1417–1450. For a detailed discussion of its dating, see E. Demougeot, "La *Notitia Dignitatum* et l'histoire de l'Empire d'Occident au debut du Vme siècle," *Latomus* 34 (1975), 1079–1134, and Berger, pp. 41, 143, 158–59.

brightly decorated shields which belonged to commanders of military units[3] (figs. 1 and 2).

Insignia uiri illustris magistri officiorum.

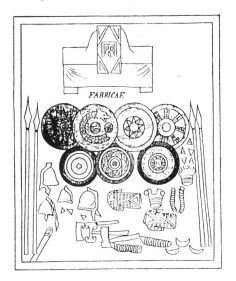 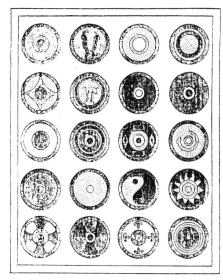

Figs. 1–2. Pages from the *Notitia dignitatum* showing illustrations of shields

What makes them particularly intriguing is that while most of these shield devices are graced with decorative elements generally known to the classical world, many display barbarian motifs[4] (fig. 3), and a few even carry designs which appear to have little or nothing in common with the iconography of the European world. Such, in particular, is the device found on the shield of the

---

[3] Berger, who is the first to have conducted a systematic analysis of all its illustrations, observes that the *Notitia dignitatum* "has rarely been treated from an art-historical perspective" (*Insignia of the Notitia Dignitatum,* p. xviii). The first to delve into the origins of Late Roman shield insignia, including some in the *Notitia,* was Andreas Alföldi with his article "Ein spätrömisches Schildzeichen keltischer oder germanischer Herkunft," *Germania* 19 (1935), 324–28. Following him, Franz Altheim attempted to demonstrate that some of the shields of the *Notitia* contained runic signs; see Franz Altheim and E. Trautmann-Nehring, *Kimbern und Runen* (Berlin, 1942), pp. 9–11, 59–60; and Franz Altheim, "Runen als Schildzeichen," *Klio* 31 (1938), 51–59. The only studies which address specifically the iconography of the shields in the *Notitia,* however, are a portion of Berger's own work (pp. 43–57) and the two articles by Grigg: "Portrait-Bearing Codicils?" and "Inconsistency and Lassitude: The Shield Emblems of the *Notitia Dignitatum,*" *Journal of Roman Studies* 73 (1983), 132–42.

[4] The bright primary colors reflect Tacitus' observation (*Germania* 6) that the Germans took great pride in their shields, which they decorated with select colors. Many of the shields in the *Notitia* are decorated with what appear to be impaled heads, and some have been thought to contain runes (see n. 3).

Armigeri (*Oc*. V, 78)[5] (fig. 4) and the identical though less attractively executed example on the shield of the *Mauriosismiaci* (*Oc*. V, 118) (fig. 5).

Fig. 3. Shield of the *Uisi* showing an impaled head

Fig. 4. *Yin-yang* symbol on the shield of the *Armigeri*

Pamela Berger, whose 1981 monograph is the most thorough art-historical study of these shield insignia to date, and who appears to be the only one, so far, to have addressed the question of the origin of the *Armigeri* shield emblem in particular, has described its "flowing curvilinearity" and "asymmetrical S-curve design" as being entirely unlike "any of the shields on Roman monuments."[6] But neither Berger nor anyone else has ventured to articulate the striking resemblance which this design bears to the familiar *yin-yang* diagram of China (fig. 6).

Fig. 5. *Yin-yang* symbol on shield of the *Mauriosismiaci*

Fig. 6. The Chinese *yin-yang* symbol

---

[5] All references to individual shields are by numbers as in the edition by Seeck, *Notitia Dignitatum*.

[6] Berger, *Insignia of the Notitia Dignitatum*, p. 57.

If the design on the *Armigeri* shield were merely similar to the Chinese diagram, then its origin could perhaps be rationalized as a coincidence resulting from artists working independently with limited options. But the circular shape, the differently colored mouchettes separated by the reverse S-curve, with the smaller circles in the thick ends of the mouchettes, make it so identical with the *yin-yang* symbol in every detail that the proposal of a common origin does not appear to be out of order. Admittedly, the likelihood of a Chinese cosmological symbol finding its way into a Roman document may appear remote, but the possibility should not be dismissed out of hand. After all, by the time the *Notitia* was being compiled, trade contacts between the Mediterranean world and China, albeit through intermediaries, had been in effect for some five hundred years.[7] Moreover, when names of such Asian peoples as the *Alani, Scythae, Armeni* and *Transtigritani* are encountered among the military units listed in the *Notitia*, there begins to emerge a mosaic of the complex cross-cultural influences that shaped the character of the late Empire. And these names are associated with shield devices whose iconographic heritage appears to have been derived from far outside the classical tradition. It is against the background of this diverse heritage that the emblem on the *Armigeri* shield must be examined.

Three arguments have been advanced in support of an independent origin of the "asymmetrical design" on the *Armigeri* shield. The first, suggested by what Berger calls the *Notitia's* "ignominious status as a copy of a copy,"[8] is that the design could have been generated as a corruption or outright invention in the process of transmission of the work from its Roman original to the Carolingian and then to the late medieval exemplars extant today. J. J. G. Alexander's careful analysis of the principal manuscripts, however, has yielded evidence of a fairly incorrupt transmission,[9] and the subsequent art-historical examination by Berger has confirmed that the iconography of the shields "has been transmitted with remarkable precision" and retains "an unexpected degree of authenticity."[10]

In the second instance, Robert Grigg, while not challenging the claims to the accuracy of transmission, has questioned whether the illustrations represent authentic Roman shield emblems in the first place.[11] He contends that "the artist's sources were so impoverished that he was reduced to relying on his own powers of invention." This is suggested by the mere repetition of designs with only slight variation, and by attempts to create variety through unconventional juxtaposition of forms.[12] Consequently, Grigg holds, although the shield emblems of the *Notitia dignitatum* have been accurately transmitted, they nevertheless are "largely *ad hoc* fabrications."[13] He concludes that one

---

[7] Joseph Needham, *Science and Civilization in China* (Cambridge, 1963), 1:170–88.

[8] Berger, *Insignia of the Notitia Dignitatum,* p. xix.

[9] Alexander, "Illustrated Manuscripts," pp. 11-25.

[10] Berger, *Insignia of the Notitia Dignitatum,* pp. 57, 168.

[11] Ibid., p. 57.

[12] Grigg, "Portrait-Bearing Codicils?" pp. 111–12.

[13] Grigg, "Inconsistency," p. 132.

may indeed, then "not expect from the illustrations of the *Notitia dignitatum* much more than a general idea of how late Roman insignia looked."[14]

The same kind of artistic impoverishment, repetition and unconventional juxtaposition of forms, however, can be found in shields portrayed on Roman mausoleums, triumphal arches, columns and other monuments dating from the Age of Augustus all the way to the early Byzantine era. The Mauretanian cavalry on Trajan's Column, for instance, carries round shields, many of which are completely devoid of decorations, as does also the trophy tree in the frieze of the triumphal procession from the Temple of Apollo Sosianus, and the statue of the Amazon from Hadrian's villa.[15] In her catalogue of the shields depicted on Trajan's Column, Flora B. Florescu has categorized all 297 examples according to shape and decorative design. Quite a few of them exhibit very simple and unimaginative decorations (figs. 7–10). Others,

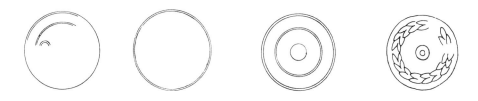

Figs. 7–10. Round shields from Trajan's Column

notably the semicylindrical ones,[16] show almost slavish repetition with very little variation, while by far the majority exhibit designs which are simply combinations of a stock of common decorative elements[17] (figs. 11–19). The same is the case with the shields on the Arc d'Orange.[18] From these examples it would appear that artistic impoverishment as well as achievement of variety in shield decorations by means of resorting to the powers of one's own imagination may not have been a proclivity of the illustrator of the *Notitia dignitatum* alone, but of the decorators of Roman monuments in general. But one must not exclude from this responsibility the craftsmen's shops which produced the original artifacts. Are they to be credited with more artistic imagination than the sculptors whose job it was to portray shields on

---

[14] Ibid., p. 112.

[15] Ranuccio Bianchi Bandinelli, *Rome the Center of Power, 500 B.C. to A.D. 200* (New York, 1970), pp. 68, 243, 274.

[16] Flora B. Florescu, *Die Trajanssäule: Grundfragen und Tafeln* (Bucharest, 1969), pp. 82–83.

[17] Ibid., pp. 71–75, 90–94. See also R. Amy, P.-M. Duval, J.-J. Hatt, A. Piganiol, Ch. Picard and G.-Ch. Picard, *L'Arc d'Orange* (Paris, 1962), Pl. 45–48.

[18] R. Amy, *L'Arc d'Orange,* pp. 45–48.

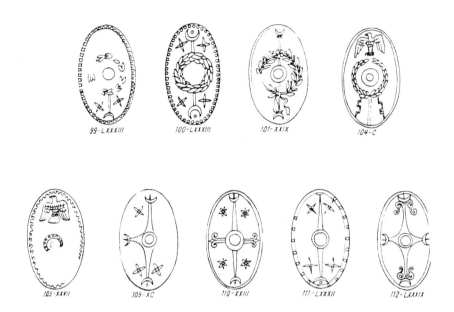

Figs. 11–19. Oval shields on Trajan's Column

impressive public monuments? Both the monuments and the *Notitia* show shields with "impoverished" decorations, shields with unimaginative repetitions of standard forms, and shields with unusual combinations and juxtapositions of forms, and the reason for this may be none other than that the shields were simply made that way. But even if, for the sake of argument, the "asymmetrical design" attributed to the *Armigeri* shield may have been placed there purely by the whim of the illustrator of the *Notitia*, it does not necessarily follow that it would have been his independent invention. Given the eclectic liberties of the writers and artists of late antiquity, he could have borrowed it from a decorated artifact of barbarian origin. The possibility that this design is merely the artist's invention is, therefore, rather remote, and the quest for its origin still valid.

Thirdly, in attempting to trace its iconographic origins, Berger has described the fluid curving lines and spiraling vocabulary displayed on the *Armigeri* shield as characteristic of Celtic art, and suggested with confidence that the design is derived from that source.[19] Admittedly, the circles, swirls, volutes, mouchettes and modified palmettes which are basic components of

---

[19] Berger, *Insignia of the Notitia Dignitatum,* p. 57. Only one work on Celtic art is cited.

Celtic decorative art do contain, although not too frequently, an element which resembles the design on the above shield[20] (figs. 20–23). Several

Figs. 20–23. Celtic artifacts with decorations resembling the *yin-yang* design

scholars have even used the term *yin-yang* in reference to it[21] (figs. 24–28). This similarity, however, is deceptive. Of the Celtic examples cited by

---

[20] See examples in Henri Hubert, *The Rise of the Celts* (New York, 1934), p. 124 fig. 24; Stuart Piggott, *Ancient Europe* (Chicago, 1965), p. 242 figs. 135, 136.2; Duncan Norton-Taylor, *The Celts* (New York, 1974), p. 60; Paul Jacobsthal, *Early Celtic Art,* 2 vols. (Oxford, 1944), 1:78 and 2:pl. 117, 271 nos. 310, 312; Germain Bazin, *The Loom of Art* (New York, 1962), pp. 154–55.

[21] Sir Cyril Fred Fox, *Pattern and Purpose* (Cardiff, 1958), pp. 148–49 no. 52; Jacobsthal, *Early Celtic Art* 2:pl. 312; Bazin, loc. cit. See also Marija Gimbutas, *The Gods and Goddesses of Old Europe* (Berkeley, 1974), pp. 172, 174 for resemblances to *yin-yang* type of designs in Neolithic Eastern Europe.

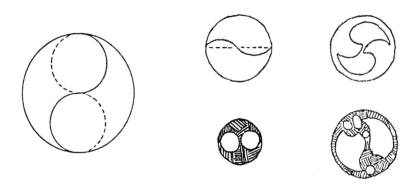

Figs. 24–28. "Yin-yang"–like motifs found in Celtic art

Berger,[22] the shield boss actually shows interlocking stylized bird heads[23] (fig. 29) which bear only an approximate resemblance to the *Armigeri* shield, the design on the linchpin shows the two embossed circles within an otherwise dissimilar pattern (fig. 30), and the Mayer mirror displays, around a profusion

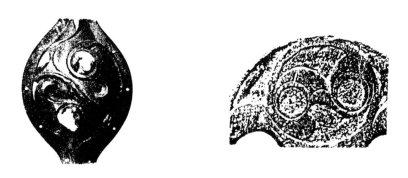

Fig. 29. Boss from the Wandsworth shield showing   Fig. 30. Celtic linchpin
         interlocking stylized birds' heads

---

[22] Fox, *Pattern and Purpose,* pp. 146–50, plates 55, 57. Berger's examination appears to have been rather cursory.

[23] N. K. Sandars, *Prehistoric Art in Europe* (Baltimore, 1968), p. 261, pl. 288.

of circles set in cam-shaped designs and intersecting volutes, large forward and reverse S-curves which actually lend the entire composition the opposite of asymmetry[24] (fig. 31). This element, however, is mostly found in La Tène art, which had disappeared by late Roman times. Furthermore, rather than stand as an independent motif, in early Celtic art this "yin-yang" design, as Jacobsthal has pointed out,[25] always appears only as an integral component of a larger pattern. This is also the case with the designs in such examples of late Celtic art as the elaborately illum-inated pages of the *Book of Dar-*

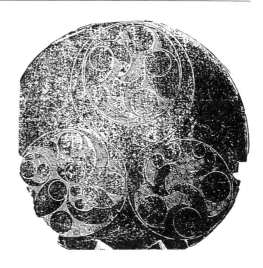

Fig. 31. The Mayer mirror

row (fig. 32) and the *Book of Kells* (fig. 33), which are early medieval works.[26] To these examples might also be added the decorations on the mirror

Fig. 32. Illumination from the *Book of Darrow*

---

[24] The Desborough mirror may have been a more appropriate example to cite. See T. G. E. Powell, "Barbarian Europe: From the First Farmers to the Celts," in *The Dawn of Civilization,* ed. Stuart Piggott (New York, 1961), p. 347.

[25] Jacobsthal, *Early Celtic Art* 1:78.

[26] Norton-Taylor, *The Celts,* pp. 133, 139.

from the Sutton Hoo treasure[27] (fig. 34). On the other hand, surviving illustrations of Celtic shields show them as either utterly devoid of decorations, or else graced with simple palmettes around the center and extremities of a plain longitudinal rib[28] (figs. 35–37).

Fig. 33. Illumination from the *Book of Kells*   Fig. 34. Sutton Hoo mirror with *yin-yang* type of decoration (inset)

Such paucity of decoration is evident on the *Celtae iuniores* shield in the *Notitia* (*Oc.* V, 56) (fig. 38). Even the famous Battersea Shield (fig. 39), with its three vertically arranged circles, is closer in resemblance to the emblem on the *Notitia* shield of the Celtic *Gallicani* (*Oc.* V, 98) (fig. 40) than to that of the *Armigeri.*[29] When these and other details are considered, the connection between the device on the *Armigeri* shield and Celtic art appears tenuous at best.

As has been already demonstrated, however, there is a remarkably close resemblance between the design on the *Armigeri* shield and the double-tadpole *yin-yang* symbol of China. In Chinese tradition this diagram, with its

[27] Magnus Backes and Regine Dölling, *Art of the Dark Ages,* trans. Francisca Garvie (New York, 1969), p. 46.

[28] Jacobsthal, *Early Celtic Art* plate 216 a, c; Norton-Taylor, *The Celts,* p. 116; Piggott, *Ancient Europe,* plate 43.

[29] Hubert, *Rise of the Celts,* p. 126; Norton-Taylor, *The Celts,* p. 53.

Figs. 35–37. Celtic shields

Fig. 38. Shield of the
Celtae iuniores

Fig. 41. *Yin-yang*
symbol on a Chinese lacquer plaque

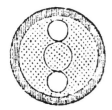

Fig. 40. Shield of the
Gallicani

Fig. 39. Battersea Shield

differently colored interlocking halves, portrays the interrelationship of two opposing universal elements, forces or principles which are necessary for the maintenance of cosmic order[30] (fig. 41). The origins of this *yin-yang* concept

---

[30] Wing-Tsit Chan, trans. and ed., *A Source Book in Chinese Philosophy* (Princeton, 1963), pp. 244–45; Needham, *Science and Civilization* (1969), 2:276–78. For a graphic

can be traced back to before the third century B.C., and it had become well
known by Han times (206 B.C.–220 A.D.). The graphic diagram itself,
however, is much more recent, and little has been done to ascertain its origin.
Joseph Needham, indeed, deplored the fact that no monograph has been
written on the developmental history of this symbol.[31] The earliest diagram
known to him in 1977 was that of a spiral-shaped *yin-yang* symbol contained
in a collection of writings and charts compiled in 1613[32] (figs. 42–43). There

Figs. 42–43. Early version of a *yin-yang* symbol in a seventeenth-century Chinese
manuscript and on a more recent statue of a Lohan

is also a very beautiful but slightly later example on a seventeenth-century silk
scroll[33] (fig. 44). More recently, as pointed out by the late Professor Lynn
White, Jr., a ninth-century example has been discovered in China.[34] Thus, the
illustration on the *Armigeri* shield would appear to be the oldest known
graphic example of the *yin-yang* symbol in existence. Of course, neither the
Notitia dignitatum, nor for that matter any other Roman document, betrays
even the remotest familiarity with the *yin-yang* cosmology; the symbol on the
shield is all there is.

---

example of this diagram, see the example from a lacquer plaque in Thomas Froneck, ed.,
Horizon Book of the Arts of China (New York, 1969), p. 38.

[31] Needham, *Science and Civilization* (Cambridge, 1980), 5/4:379 note c.

[32] Joseph Needham, "The Institute's Symbol," *Biologist* 24 (May, 1977), 71–72; *Science
and Civilization* (1983), 5/5:230.

[33] Gildo Fossati, *China,* trans. Bruce Penman, The Monuments of Civilization (London,
1983), p. 22.

[34] Personal communication of January 12, 1984 to the author.

But the *Armigeri* shield is not the only one that bears a symbol suggestive of oriental origins. The same design, as pointed out earlier, occurs also on the shield of the *Mauriosismiaci* (*Oc.* V, 118) (fig. 5), and modified forms of it are portrayed on the shields of the *Ascarii seniores* (*Or.* IX, 3) (fig. 45), the *Primarii* and *Undecimani* (*Or.* VI, 5, 6) (figs. 46–47), and the *Martenses seniores* (*Or.* VII, 5) (fig. 48). All these appear to be variants of that same *yin* and *yang* design.

Of vital significance in this regard is yet another shield with a non-classical design. Ascribed to the unit of the *Thebei* (*Oc.* V, 11) (fig. 49), it consists

Fig. 44. *Yin-yang* symbol on a seventeenth-century silk scroll

Fig. 45. Shield of the *Ascarii seniores*

Fig. 48. Shield of the *Martenses seniores*

Figs. 46–47. Shields of the *Primarii* and *Undecimani*

of three concentric circles bisected by a vertical line, the resulting semicircular sectors being rendered in alternating light and dark colors. This device is definitely not Celtic, but it is one which yet again has an exact counterpart in China: the *T'ai-chi* or Great Ultimate. The *I Ching*, a book dating from the third century B.C., and possibly much earlier, characterizes the Great Ultimate as the beginning of everything, which engendered the *yin* and *yang*, out of the interaction of which two forces, in turn, all ideas, systems, patterns and culture have come forth.[35] The earliest known graphic representation of it, however, is found in the eighth-century Taoist book, *Shang Feng Ta Tung-Chen Yuan Miao Thu* ("Diagrams of the Mysterious Cosmic Classic of the T'ung Chen Scriptures").[36] Subsequently the scholar Chou Tun-i (1017–1073) described it in a short essay, *Thai Chi Thu* ("Diagram of the Supreme Pole"), accompanied by an illustration[37] (fig. 50). This is, then, a second Chinese cosmological symbol represented in the iconography of the *Notitia dignitatum*.

Fig. 49. Shield of the *Thebei*   Fig. 50. Eleventh-century diagram of the
                                        Thai Chi or Supreme Pole

Among the quadruped motifs represented on the shields of the *Notitia* are some of what appear to be wolves. To the Romans, of course, the wolf figured prominently in the legendary origins of their city. But whereas some shields depicted on Roman monuments display the scene of the mother wolf nursing the infant Romulus and Remus[38] (figs. 51–52), such traditional lupine iconography is absent from the *Notitia*. Here, instead, are emblems of what appear to be wolf-headed flagpole finials (*Or.* VI, 16, 18; *Oc.* V, 38) (figs.

35 Chan, *Source Book in Chinese Philosophy,* pp. 262–63; E. T. C. Werner, *A Dictionary of Chinese Mythology* (Shanghai, 1932), pp. 478–80.

36 Needham, *Science and Civilization* (1969), 2:467–68.

37 Ibid., pp. 459–61. The design in the *Notitia* lacks the central hole of the Chinese diagram. This would have been represented by the boss of the shield, which in this case the artist did not include.

38 Florescu, *Die Trajanssäule,* p. 75 nos. 102–3; cf. Berger, *Insignia of the Notitia Dignitatum,* p. 52; Bandinelli, *Rome,* p. 287, where, on the base of the Column of Antoninus Pius, Rome is shown leaning on a round shield sporting a relief of the wolf and the twins.

53–55) with two heads confronting each other in a heraldic posture,[39] and scenes of wolves running, as if on a hunt (*Or.* V, 23; VIII, 3, 6) (figs. 56–58). This represents a different kind of wolf tradition, one which is closer to ancient Chinese and Scythian art or the blue wolf totem of Turkic legend.[40]

Figs. 51–52. Roman shields
with traditional lupine
iconography

Figs. 53–55. Shields with wolf headed finials

Figs. 56–58. Shields with running wolves

Also associated with wolf motifs are a number of shields showing composite creatures with wolf heads and serpentine bodies (*Oc.* VI, 16, 22, 35, 36; *Or.* XI, 3) (figs. 59–63), one of them scaly (*Oc.* IX, 3) (fig. 64). They

---

[39] The earliest known examples of similar finials are found among the Luristan bronzes, although there the animals are ibexes and panthers. See P. R. S. Moorey, Emma C. Bunker, Edith Paroda and Glenn Markoe, *Ancient Bronzes, Ceramics and Seals* (Los Angeles, 1981), pp. 52–55.

[40] The running dog as an ornament in Han dynasty art is pointed out by Käte Finsterbusch, *Verzeichnis und Motivindex der Han Darstellungen* (Wiesbaden, 1966), 1:227; a connection between the wolf (on the shield of the *Tertiodecimanes* a blue wolf) and the blue wolf totem of the Turks was suggested already by Alföldi, "Ein spätrömisches Schildzeichen," pp. 327–8.

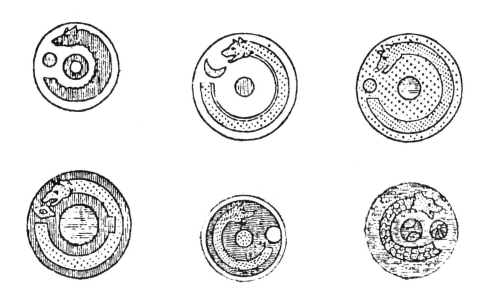

Figs. 59–64. Shields with dragons

have ears raised, mouth open, nose and lip upturned.[41] Such lupine-
dracontine monsters were known to the Romans from their dragon
standards.[42] A metallic open-jawed canine head with snarling upper lip and
bared fangs was carried on top of a pole, to which was attached a tubular cloth
"body" of the creature in such a manner that it would inflate and writhe in
the wind.[43] This device did not actually originate with the Romans, but was
adopted by them from their barbarian enemies and military auxiliaries:
dragon banners captured from the Dacians are featured on reliefs at the base
of Trajan's Column, while others appear on the remains of Hadrian's tomb
and on the sarcophagus of one of Marcus Aurelius' generals[44] (figs. 65–67).
The Dacians appear to have borrowed it from their Sarmatian allies, an
equestrian people from Central Asia who had invaded southeastern Europe in
the last two centuries B.C. A stone relief in Chester, England, shows a mounted

---

[41] For detail of a Roman sculpture depicting such a wolf-headed dragon, see Peter Croft,
Roman Mythology (London, 1974), p. 37.

[42] Flavius Vegetius Renatus, *De re militari* 13 (Strassbourg, 1556), p. 42.

[43] J. S. P. Tatlock, "The "Dragons of Wessex," and Wales," *Speculum* 8 (1933), 223.

[44] Lino Rossi, *Trajan's Column and the Dacian Wars,* trans. J. M. C. Toynbee (London,
1971), p. 126; Ernest Nash, *Pictorial Dictionary of Ancient Rome,* 2 vols. (New York, 1961),
1:459 pl. 562; and Bandinelli, *Rome,* p. 305 pl. 345. See also Sergei J. Rudenko, "The
Mythological Eagle, the Gryphon, the Winged Lion, and the Wolf in the Art of the Northern
Nomads," *Artibus Asiae* 21 (1958), 119.

Sarmatian auxiliary carrying this type of dragon banner[45] (fig. 68). The earliest known examples of such banners come actually from the discoveries at Pazyryk[46] (fourth century B.C.) and Noin Ula[47] (second century B.C.) of wooden wolf-headed effigies with holes underneath for mounting on poles, and accompanying silk tubular banners with "scales" and "limbs" sewn on to simulate the "body" of the monster (figs. 69–71). Similar banners were used by the Parthians and various Turkic peoples of Central Asia[48] (figs. 72–73). In Europe such dragon banners survived into medieval times.

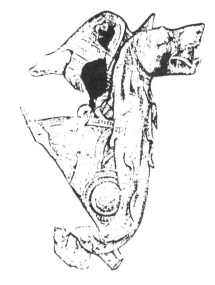

Figs. 65–67. Dragon banners on Roman monuments

---

[45] Helmut Nickel, "The Dawn of Chivalry," in The Metropolitan Museum of Art, *From the Lands of the Scythians: Ancient Treasures From the Museums of the U.S.S.R. 3000 B.C.–100 B.C.* (New York, 1976), p. 151.

[46] Emel Esin, "Tös and Moncuk: Notes on Turkish Flag-Pole Finials," *Central Asiatic Journal* 16 (1972), 14–36.

[47] Sergei J. Rudenko, *Die Kultur der Hsiung-nu und die Hügelgräber von Noin Ula,* trans. Helmut Pollems (Bonn, 1969), pp. 68, 74, plate 32.2.

[48] Esin, "Tös and Moncuk," pp. 14–15, 22.

Fig. 68. Sarmatian rider with dragon
banner from Chester, England

Figs. 69–71. Dragon banners from Pazyryk and Noin Ula

King Arthur is credited with having carried one, its use by Carolingian cavalry is attested in the *Psalterium Aureum* of St. Gall (fig. 74), and Harold Godwinson flew a pair of them at the Battle of Hastings[49] (fig. 75).

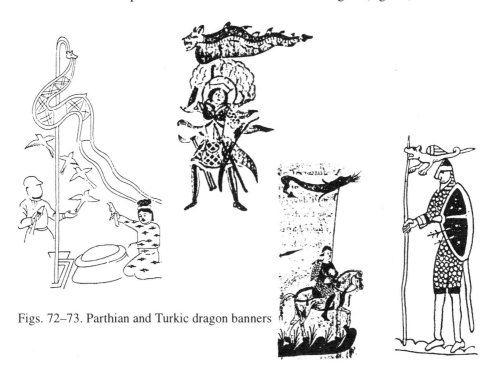

Figs. 72–73. Parthian and Turkic dragon banners

Fig. 74. Carolingian
horseman with
dragon banner

Fig. 75. Anglo-Saxon
with dragon banner
on Bayeux Tapestry

In the *Notitia*, however, the emblems with the lupine dragons exhibit features not found with the Sarmatian or Roman banners. First of all, the creature is curled in a circle around the inner perimeter of the shield, with its nose close to its tail. Almost identical tail-eating serpent images can be seen on coins of the Boii (fig. 76) which are near contemporaries of the *Notitia*.[50] Toward the East such curled animal motifs, mostly of panthers, are well represented in Scythian art[51] (figs. 77–80), but the origin of the style can be

---

[49] Tatlock, "Dragons of Wessex," pp. 227, 229; Backes and Dölling, *Art of the Dark Ages,* p. 118.

[50] Alföldi, "Ein spätrömisches Schildzeichen," p. 328.

[51] *From the Lands of the Scythians,* pp. 43, 103, 105–6; Tamara Talbot Rice, *Ancient Arts of Central Asia* (New York, 1965), p. 74; Altheim, "Runen als Schildzeichen," p. 52.

traced back to dragon decorations on the Shang bronzes of China[52] (figs. 81–85). A carved jade ring of the Chou period, now in the British Museum, displays a curled dragon (fig. 86) which is almost identical in form to those on the shields of the *Notitia* and on the Boii coins[53] (figs. 59–64, 76). A similar figure is also found in a Han dynasty jade dragon[54] (fig. 87).

Fig. 76. Coiled serpent
on Boii coin

Figs. 77–80. Curled animals in Scythian art

Figs. 81–85. Curled dragon decorations from Shang bronzes

---

[52] Bernhard Karlgren, "Notes on the Grammar of Early Bronze Decor," *Bulletin of the Museum of Far Eastern Antiquities* 23 (Stockholm, 1951), 1–37 and figs. 30–34, 38; Needham, *Science and Civilization* (1983), 5:381. On examples of "tail biting" (i.e. curled) dragons in Han times, see Finsterbusch, *Verzeichnis und Motivindex* 1:227.

[53] Needham, *Science and Civilization* (1980), 5/4:381–3 and especially fig. 1528a.

[54] Ting Sing Wu, ed., *Treasures of China,* vol. 2 (Taipei, 1970), p. 40.

Fig. 86. Chou dynasty carved jade ring
in the form of a curled dragon

Fig. 87. Curled jade dragon
from the Han dynasty

But in the *Notitia*, also, the curled serpent or dragon, with pricked ears and open jaw is in several instances depicted facing or chasing either a sphere, crescent moon or diamond-shaped object[55] (figs. 59–64). The earliest parallel to this comes again from Pazyryk, from a tattoo in which a dragon-headed creature, nose and lip upturned in a snarl, is playing with or about to devour a number of round objects[56] (fig. 88). Emel Esin calls this the dragon-and-pearl motif, and cites examples of its occurrence among the Turkic peoples, who portrayed a wolf with a pearl between its teeth[57] (fig. 89).

Fig. 88. Beast with round objects, from Pazyryk

Fig. 89. Turkic metal plaque of
wolf with pearl between its teeth

---

[55] Berger, *Insignia of the Notitia Dignitatum*, p. 56.
[56] Sergei J. Rudenko, *The Frozen Tombs of Siberia*, trans. M. W. Thompson (Berkeley, 1970), p. 262.
[57] Esin, "Tös and Moncuk," pp. 27–30.

By Han times the dragon-and-pearl motif had also become established in China, as is evident from a bronze handle with two dragon heads (fig. 90) and a tomb relief of a dragon playing with a *pi* disc[58] (fig. 91). The *pi*, like the pearl and the jewel, was a symbol for a celestial body and had powerful cosmological significance when associated with the dragon.[59] The famous scientist Chang Heng (78–139) used balls dropped out of the mouths of dragons as indicators in his directional seismometer[60] (fig. 92). Eventually the dragon and pearl became a ubiquitous element in Chinese art, and can be found on paintings, porcelain, apparel and flags (fig. 93).

Figs. 90–91. Han dynasty dragons with pearls and *pi* disc

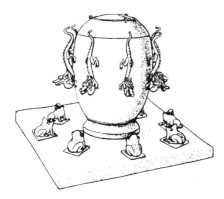 

Fig. 92. Chang Heng's seismometer   Fig. 93. Modern Chinese emblem
        with dragons and balls   with dragon and pearl

---

[58] Chêng Tê-K'un, *Archaeological Studies in Szechwan* (Cambridge, Mass., 1967), plates 68.25 and 72.3; Finsterbusch, *Verzeichnis und Motivindex* 2:34, 234; Needham, *Science and Civilization* 3:252.

[59] Cf. Needham, *Science and Civilization* (1970), 3:252; also Werner, *Dictionary of Chinese Mythology,* p. 288. This may explain why in the *Notitia* the dragon is associated with a sphere, a moon, or a jewel. The symbolism of these objects is the same.

[60] Needham, *Science and Civilization* (1970), 3:626–28.

With these tail-eating pearl-chasing dragons has emerged, then, a third instance in which a device on the shields of the *Notitia dignitatum* has been found to have demonstrable iconographic correspondence with a Chinese cosmic symbol.

In addition to the *yin-yang*, *T'ai-chi* and dragon emblems, the shields of the *Notitia* contain still other devices with apparent eastern iconographic connections.[61] Prevalent are wheels with multiple spokes (*Or.* V, 2; VI, 7; VIII, 9; IX, 2; *Oc.* V, 93, 103; VI, 11)[62] (figs. 94–100) which resemble a Parthian solar disc[63] (fig. 101). Two shields with a radiating herringbone design

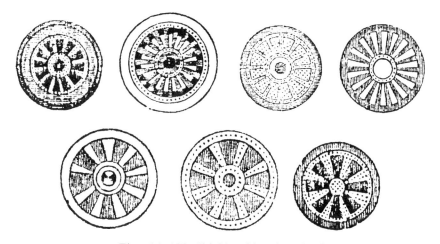

Figs. 94–100. Shields with solar wheels

---

[61] Some shields, which will not be discussed here in detail, display designs suggesting a Middle Eastern heritage. The star on the shield of the *Fortenses auxiliarii* (*Or.* VII, 15), for instance, is identical to one often found on Assyrian and Babylonian reliefs; see Ilse Fuhr, *Ein altorientalisches Symbol* (Wiesbaden, 1967), p. 14 no. 16. The sun symbol on an Assyrian shield (Pierre Amiet, *Art of the Ancient Near East*, trans. John Shepley and Claude Choquet [New York, 1980], p. 404 plate 591) resembles several examples in the *Notitia* (Oc. V, 79; Or. XI, 2, 4), while an Assyrian standard (Eugène Goblet d'Aviella, *The Migration of Symbols* [New York, 1894], p. 230 and fig. 131) is suggested to be a prototype of Roman designs like those which Grigg regards as the juxtaposed emblems ("Portrait-Bearing Codicils," p. 112; cf. Or. VII, 11, 12; VIII, 21). The existence of units with such oriental names as the *Comaginenses* (*Oc.* V, 110), *Armeni* (*Or.* VI, 31; VII, 13, 14, 49, 50), *Palmirenses* (*Or.* VII, 34), *Parthi* (*Or.* V, 40; VII, 19, 32, 55; *Oc.* VI, 25, 30) and even the *Transtigritani* (*Or.* VII, 22) may account at least in part for these similarities.

[62] Berger (*Insignia of the Notitia Dignitatum,* p. 40) sees the spokes as lances or arrows, but the arrows which decorate the shields on Trajan's Column have a much different appearance (Florescu, *Die Trajanssäule,* p. 72).

[63] Talbot Rice, *Ancient Arts,* p. 86. A similar radiating solar design is to be found on the shields on a silver dish of Theodosius I, dating from 388 (John Beckwith, *The Art of Constantinople* [London, 1961], p. 17).

(*Or*. VII, 6, 7) (fig. 102–103) bear close similarity to Sogdian shields in a combat scene on a late Sassanid silver plate[64] (fig. 104). Among the many images of flagpole finials are some with heraldic wolf heads (*Or*. VI, 16, 18; *Oc*. V, 38) (figs. 53–55), heads of serpents (*Or*. VII, 19; *Oc*. V, 17; VI, 4) (figs. 105–107), and possibly also birds (*Or*. VI, 9)[65] (fig. 108), all of which have their parallels in the Sarmatian symbol of the bird on the pole[66] (fig. 109), finials of heraldic birds found from Rome and Scythia to Korea[67] (figs. 110–115), two dragon heads

Fig. 101. Parthian silver plate with solar wheel

in a late example of an emblem carried by Timur (fig. 116), and even a pair of heraldic serpents on an eighteenth-century Persian leather shield[68] (fig. 117). There is also close similarity between the crescent-shaped finials depicted on shields of the *Notitia* (*Or*. VIII, 21; *Oc*. V, 14–16) and examples from Assyria and Central Asia[69] (figs. 118–123). Two *Notitia* shields have serpents with bodies that look like ropes (*Oc*. V, 75, 96) (figs. 124–125), which are reminiscent of the Turkish practice of referring to snakes as ropes.[70] In addition to the connections with China, then, the shields of the *Notitia* also have links with Central Asia. But it remains yet to be established by what paths and means these Asian iconographic traditions could have reached the Roman Empire.

---

[64] Ibid., p. 40.

[65] It is difficult to identify the heads on the *Cornuti* shield; they appear to be birds. A similar design on a marble bust of Commodus (Bandinelli, *Rome*, p. 295 plate 331) shows heads of what appear to be phoenixes. Judging from what appears to be a remaining fringe of neck feathers, such birds' heads also appear to have decorated the now broken off parts of the pelta in the statue of the Amazon from Hadrian's villa (Ibid., p. 274 pl. 309).

[66] H. Vetters, "Der Vogel auf der Stange,—ein Kultsymbol," in *Atti del Convegno di Pavia per lo studio del Alto Medio Evo* (Bari, 1954), pp. 125–26.

[67] Choi Sunu, *5000 Years of Korean Art* (Seoul, 1979), p. 156 no. 177; *From the Lands of the Scythians,* p. 115; Karl Jettmar, *Art of the Steppes,* trans. Ann E. Keep (New York, 1969), p. 79.

[68] Donald Chaput, "The Art of the Asian Armorer," *Terra* 25/3 (Jan./Feb., 1987), 12.

[69] Esin, "Tös and Moncuk," plate VIIe. For the Assyrian standard, see Eliezer D. Oren, "Ziklag: A Biblical City on the Edge of the Negev," *Biblical Archeologist* 45 (1982), 160.

[70] Esin, "Tös and Moncuk," pp. 17, 24.

Figs. 102–3. Shields with
radiating herringbone design

Fig. 104. Sogdian silver plate showing shields with
radiating herringbone design

Figs. 105–7. Shields with heraldic serpent heads

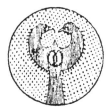

Fig. 108. Shield with
heraldic bird heads

Fig. 109. Sarmatian *tamga*
of a bird on a pole

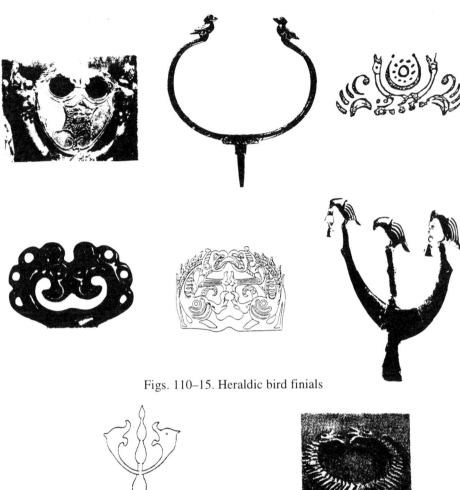

Figs. 110–15. Heraldic bird finials

Fig. 116. Dragon-headed flagpole
finial of Timur

Fig. 117. Heraldic serpents
on Persian shield

Figs. 118–21. Shields with crescent-shaped flagpole finials

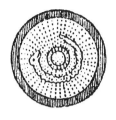

Figs. 122–23. Assyrian and Turkic   Figs. 124–25. Shields with
crescent-shaped flagpole finials   rope-like serpents

By the time that the *Notitia dignitatum* was being prepared, the Eurasian continent had been experiencing several centuries of a gradual drifting of nomadic equestrian peoples from the borders of China toward Europe. Among the earliest were the Sarmatian tribes, who began to arrive in Southern Russia in the third century B.C.; elements of them eventually ended up even in such faraway places as Spain, Brittany and the border of Scotland.

The Sarmatians are responsible for having brought with them such innovations as the long cavalry sword and scale armor,[71] and most likely also the tubular dragon-banner, all of which are to be seen among captured equipment on such monuments as the columns of Trajan and Marcus Aurelius (figs. 65–67). But although the Sarmatians had come from the borders of China and are considered to be the ones who also introduced the Chinese jade scabbard slide to western Asia and Europe,[72] they appear as unlikely candidates for having transmitted the cosmological symbols found on the shields in the *Notitia*. No dragon-and-pearl motif is to be found among captured Sarmatian equipment portrayed on Roman monuments, nor among the objects recovered from Sarmatian graves. This combination of symbols, then, must have been unknown to them when the easternmost of their tribes, the Wu-sun and the Yüeh-chih, were expelled from Central Asia and pushed westward by the Huns in the second century B.C.

Much later than the Sarmatians, appearing on the scene only some twenty years before the *Notitia* was compiled, came the Huns.[73] For centuries they

---

[71] John Eadie, "The Development of Roman Mailed Cavalry," *Journal of Roman Studies* 57 (1967), 165; William Trousdale, *The Long Sword and Scabbard Slide in Asia* (Washington, D. C., 1975), p. 112.

[72] E. Loubo-Lesnitchenko, "Imported Mirrors in the Minusinsk Basin," *Artibus Asiae* 35 (1973), 28–29; Trousdale, *The Long Sword,* pp. 109, 118.

[73] The Huns were associated, in some way which is not yet clear, with the northern Chinese tribe of the Hsiung-nu, and these two peoples are treated here as having more or less the same

had been dwelling in close proximity to China, and the Han dynasty's expansion into Central Asia brought even the westernmost Hunnic tribes under Chinese domination and cultural influence.[74] Thus from about the beginning of the current era onward the nomadic Huns of Central Asia would have found themselves at a cultural crossroads where Turkic, Iranian, Indian and Chinese influences met. Small wonder, then, that, as Justine Randers-Pehrson so graphically puts it, they arrived in Europe on horses branded with Turkish *tamgas,* carting along with them in their Chinese style wagons wives who wore Indian and Pontic jewelry and cooked food in Chinese cauldrons.[75] Chinese Central Asia would also have been the place where the Huns acquired various oriental cosmological symbols of the type that grace the shields of the *Notitia dignitatum,* whether they understood their meaning or not.

Soon after the time that the Huns arrived in Europe, about the year 375, there appeared among the Germanic barbarians a new type of fibula, or brooch, which rapidly grew in popularity, and examples of which have been found in burials from the Volga to Scandinavia and the Iberian peninsula. Its stylized dragon design (fig. 126), insists Herbert Kühn, could only have been derived from China, and it must have been brought to the West by the Huns.[76]

Further evidence of Hun culture having adopted some Chinese ways can be seen in the case of the Roman general Litorius, whose Hunnic auxiliaries divined his defeat at the hands of the Visigoths at Toulouse by reading oracle bones in the manner of the Chinese. Priscus, also, reports that in the invasion of Gaul in June, 451, Attila had his shaman divine the future by examining cracks in the shoulder blades of sheep.[77] When Attila died, he was buried in a manner conforming to the custom of the Hsiung-nu.[78] Such actions, as Randers-Pehrson has pointed out, reflect "practices that had come down to Attila from ancient days when his ancestors ranged the Chinese borderlands."[79]

In burials of the Sarmato-Hunnic period, distributed across northern Eurasia from China to the Volga, have been found Han dynasty bronze mirrors. Whether these had been brought along from the East by the Huns, or

culture. See, for instance, Omeljan Pritsak, "*Xun,* der Volksname der Hsiung-nu," *Central Asiatic Journal* 4 (1959), 27–34.

[74] Arthur Cottrell and David Morgan, *China's Civilization: A Survey of Its History, Arts, and Technology* (New York, 1975), pp. 64–65. The Hsiung-nu, for example, adopted a form of sword worship from the Chinese. See Kao Chü-hsün, "The Ching Lu Shen Shrines of Han Sword Worship in Hsiung Nu Religion," *Central Asian Journal* 5 (1960), 221–32.

[75] Justine Davis Randers-Pehrson, *Romans and Barbarians: The Birth-Struggle of Europe A.D. 400–700* (Norman, Okla., 1983), pp. 46–47.

[76] Herbert Kühn, "Das Symbol des Kosmos in der Völkerwanderungszeit," *Symbolon* 3 (1962), 108–121.

[77] Jordanes, *Getica* 196; for an evaluation, see J. Otto Maenchen-Helfen, *The World of the Huns: Studies in Their History and Culture,* ed. Max Knight (Berkeley, 1973), pp. 267–70.

[78] Maenchen-Helfen, *World of the Huns,* pp. 276, 278 n. 144.

[79] Randers-Pehrson, *Romans and Barbarians,* pp. 163–4. At this very same time, too, the royal robes and ornaments worn by the Gothic kings exhibited Central Asian design (Franz Altheim, *Die Krise der Alten Welt* [Berlin, 1943], 1:102).

by some earlier people, is still a debated issue.[80] The important fact is, however, that the backs of such round mirrors are decorated with a variety of Chinese cosmological symbols, most of which have some bearing on China's place in the universe[81] (fig. 127). Some Han mirrors, though not necessarily any of the examples found in the West, carry inscriptions referring to, among other things, the principle of *yin* and *yang*. One such example from the first century reads:

> This imperial mirror from the Shang-fang (state workshops) is wholly
>   flawless:
> Dragon on the east and Tiger on the west ward off ill luck;
> Scarlet Bird and Sombre Warrior accord with Yin andYang.[82]

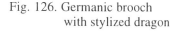

Fig. 126. Germanic brooch
    with stylized dragon

Fig. 127. Han dynasty
    bronze TLV mirror

Another, dating from 174 A.D., has the round central knob displaying in low relief two stylized animals with bodies coiled[83] (fig. 128) like the interlocking brackets on the shield of the *Ascarii seniores* in the *Notitia* (*Or.* IX, 3) (fig. 45). In the center, between the animals, are four "silkworm"

---

[80] Trousdale, *The Long Sword,* p. 112.

[81] Schuyler Cammann, "The 'TLV' Pattern on Cosmic Mirrors of the Han Dynasty," *Journal of the American Oriental Society* 68 (1948), 159–67.

[82] Needham, *Science and Civilization* (1970), 3:pl. XXXVII.

[83] A. Bulling, *The Decoration of Mirrors of the Han Period: A Chronology* (Ascone, 1960), p. 76.

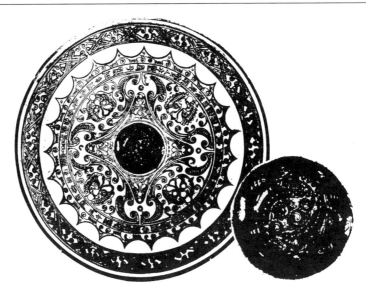

Fig. 128. Han dynasty bronze mirror with interlocking brackets on knob (inset)

scrolls, each identical in form to what later appears as a prototype version of the *yin-yang* diagram[84] (figs. 42–43). A still later mirror (600–900), with a tiger and a dragon in the center representing *yin* and *yang*, even has an inscription which specifically states that "the mutual endowments of Yin and Yang [are present in it]."[85] Whoever brought such mirrors from China to the Volga steppes may not have understood the symbolism of the decorations they bore. But the fact remains that objects of the type which sometimes bore cosmological symbols were brought to the West not so many years before the composition of the *Notitia dignitatum*. A. Bulling, who has studied such mirrors and their chronology in detail, has drawn attention to the fact that whereas the earlier examples were decorated with designs which were intended to enhance cosmological speculations, those of the third century and later were believed to possess supernatural powers and were accordingly utilized as protective charms.[86] Seen in this context, it may not have been a big step for some of the invading barbarians to have transferred the graphic symbols of such protective charms from the backs of their Chinese mirrors to the faces of their warriors' shields.

By the year 388, shortly before the eastern portion of the *Notitia dignitatum* was compiled, the Huns were not only making raids into the Empire, but elements of Hunnish auxiliaries were also serving in the army of

---

84 Needham, *Science and Civilization* (1983), 5/5:36, 230.

85 Ibid., pl. XXII.

86 Bulling, *Decoration of Mirrors,* pp. 102–4.

Emperor Theodosius; they did so again in 394.[87] In 423 Aetius brought 60,000 Huns into Gaul.[88] Subsequently units of them were integrated into the Roman forces as regular *milites*, and there is record of Huns serving in such diversified regions of the Empire as Lybia, the Danubian provinces, Gaul, and possibly even in Britain at Hadrian's wall.[89] As auxiliaries, Maenchen-Helfen has pointed out, they were obliged to furnish their own equipment.[90] Whatever standards or insignia they may have brought with them from Asia would, thus, have been carried into battle on behalf of Rome.[91] The Huns would, then, appear as the most likely ones to have appropriated Chinese and other insignia during their sojourn in Eastern and Central Asia, and at the end of their migration to have brought them to the awareness of the Romans when they fought against them and especially when units of Hun auxiliaries entered Roman military service. Seen in this perspective, the appearance of the *yin-yang* diagram on the *Armigeri* shield, drawn only some twenty years after the arrival of the Huns in the West, could hardly be mere coincidence.

In his book on the Huns, Maenchen-Helfen also addressed the question of why the *Notitia dignitatum* would have listed various barbarian units by their tribal names, among them the *Sarmati*, *Alani* and *Scythae*, but made no mention of the Huns. His conclusion was that usually the Huns were not allowed to serve together, but were distributed among various units of barbarian cavalry, archers and *armigeri*.[92] This would mean that one of the units recorded in the *Notitia dignitatum* as bearing the *yin-yang* insignia may indeed have been composed of the very people who brought that same emblem, as well as the dragon-and-pearl motif and the *T'ai-chi*, from the Great Wall of China to the *limes* of the Late Roman Empire.

LOS ANGELES VALLEY COLLEGE

---

[87] Maenchen-Helfen, *World of the Huns,* pp. 71, 248; Randers-Pehrson, *Romans and Barbarians,* p. 69. Randers-Pehrson points out (p. 78) that by this time the Roman soldiers were dressed, like the barbarians, in breeches and heavy cloaks, and that their officers decked themselves out with massive glittering cloisonné ornaments.

[88] Randers-Pehrson, *Romans and Barbarians,* p. 131.

[89] Maenchen-Helfen, *World of the Huns,* pp. 255–57.

[90] Ibid., p. 249. Randers-Pehrson points out (*Romans and Barbarians,* p. 53) that Gratian's Alan bodyguard, for example, wore fur and carried the bow in public.

[91] Randers-Pehrson argues (*Romans and Barbarians,* p. 45) that the scale covered shield on which the Vandal Stilicho is leaning in the ivory diptych of Monza must be Hunnic, because Stilicho had a Hunnic bodyguard and because the scale pattern was a Hunnic decorative motif; see depiction in Donald Strong, *Roman Art* (Baltimore, 1976), plate 241. As attractive as this proposal may appear, however, it is invalidated by the fact that a shield with an identical design is to be found already on a relief, in the Palazzo della Cancellaria, dating from the reign of Domitian, i.e. three hundred years before the arrival of the Huns (Bandinelli, *Rome,* p. 213).

[92] Maenchen-Helfen, *World of the Huns,* p. 255.

LIST OF FIGURES

Fig. 38   Shield of the *Celtae iuniores* (Seeck, *Oc.* V, 56 [p. 117]).

Fig. 39   Battersea Shield (Hubert, p. 125 fig. 31).

Fig. 40   Shield of the *Gallicani* (Seeck, *Oc.* V, 98 [p. 119]).

Fig. 41   *Yin-yang* symbol on a Chinese lacquer plaque (Froneck, p. 38).

Figs. 42–43   Early version of a *yin-yang* symbol in a seventeenth-century Chinese manuscript and on a more recent statue of a Lohan (Needham, *Science and Civilization*, 5/5:36, 230).

Fig. 44   *Yin-yang* symbol on a seventeenth-century silk scroll (Fossati, p. 22).

Fig. 45   Shield of the *Ascarii seniores* (Seeck, *Or.* IX, 3, p. 27).

Figs. 46–47   Shields of the *Primarii* and *Undecimani* (Seeck, *Or.* VI, 5, 6 [p. 15]).

Fig. 48   Shield of the *Martenses seniores* (Seeck, *Or.* VII, 5 [p. 19]).

Fig. 49   Shield of the *Thebei* (Seeck, *Oc.* V, 11 [p.115]).

Fig. 50   Eleventh-century diagram of the *Thai Chi* or Supreme Pole (Needham, *Science and Civilization*, 2:461).

Figs. 51–52   Roman shields with traditional lupine iconography (Florescu, p. 75).

Figs. 53–55   Shields with wolf headed finials (Seeck, *Or.* VI, 16, 18 [p. 16]; *Oc.* V, 38 [p. 116]).

Figs. 56–58   Shields with running wolves (Seeck, *Or.* V, 23 [p. 12]; VIII, 3, 6, [p. 23]).

Figs. 59–64   Shields with dragons (Seeck, *Oc.* VI, 16, 22 [p. 128], 35, 36 [p. 129], IX, 3 [p. 144]; *Or.* XI, 3 [p. 31]).

Figs. 65–67   Dragon banners on Roman monuments (Rossi, p. 126 fig. 36; Nash 1:459 plate 562; Bandinelli, p. 305 plate 345).

Fig. 68   Sarmatian rider with dragon banner from Chester, England (Nickel, p. 151).

Figs. 69–71   Dragon banners from Pazyryk and Noin Ula (Esin, p. 38 plate 2ab; p. 39 plate 4a).

Figs. 72–73   Parthian and Turkic dragon banners (Esin, p. 38 plate 2d; p. 42 plate 6b).

Fig. 74   Carolingian horseman with dragon banner (Backes and Dölling, p. 118).

Fig. 75   Anglo-Saxon with dragon banner on Bayeux Tapestry.

Fig. 76   Coiled serpent on Boii coin (Alföldi, p. 328).

Figs. 77–80   Curled animals in Scythian art (*From the Lands of the Scythians*, pp. i, 43, 103, 105–6; Talbot-Rice, p. 74).

Figs. 81–85   Curled dragon decorations from Shang bronzes (Karlgren, figs. 30–34).

Fig. 86   Chou dynasty carved jade ring in the form of a curled dragon (Needham, 5/4:382–83 fig. 1528a).

Fig. 87   Curled jade dragon from the Han dynasty (Wu, 2:40).

Fig. 88   Beast with round objects, from Pazyryk (Rudenko, *Frozen Tombs*, p. 262 fig. 129).

Fig. 89   Turkic metal plaque of wolf with pearl between its teeth (Esin, p. 40 plate 4c).

Figs. 90–91   Han dynasty dragons with pearls and *pi* disc (Tê-K'un, plates 68.25, 72.3).

Fig. 92   Chang Heng's seismometer with dragons and balls (Needham, *Science and Civilization*, 3:627).

Fig. 93   Modern Chinese emblem with dragon and pearl.

Figs. 94–100   Shields with solar wheels (Seeck, *Or.* V, 2 [p. 11]; VI, 7 [p. 15]; VIII, 9 [p. 24]; IX, 2 [p. 27]; *Oc.* V, 93, 103 [p. 119]; VI, 11 [p. 128]).

Fig. 101   Parthian silver plate with solar wheel (Talbot-Rice, p. 86).

Figs. 102–3   Shields with radiating herringbone design (Seeck, *Or.* VII, 6, 7 [pp. 19, 20]).

Fig. 104   Sogdian silver plate showing shields with radiating herringbone design (Talbot-Rice, p. 40).

Figs. 105–7   Shields with heraldic serpent heads (Seeck, *Or.* VII, 19 [p. 20]; *Oc.* V, 17 [p. 115]; VI, 4 [p. 128]).

Fig. 108   Shield with heraldic bird heads (Seeck, *Or.* VI, 9 [p. 15).

Fig. 109   Sarmatian *tamga* of a bird on a pole (Vetters, p. 125).

Figs. 110–15   Heraldic bird finials (Sunu, p. 156 no. 177; Esin, p. 44 plate 8a; Jettmar, p. 79 fig. 13, p. 102 fig. 77; Bandinelli, p. 295; *From the Lands of the Scythians*, p. 115).

Fig. 116   Dragon-headed flagpole finial of Timur (Esin, p. 43 plate 7e).

Fig. 117   Heraldic serpents on Persian shield (Chaput, p. 12).

Figs. 118–21   Shields with crescent-shaped flagpole finials (Seeck, *Or.* VIII, 21 [p. 24]; *Oc.* V, 14–16 [p. 115]).

Figs. 122–23   Assyrian and Turkic crescent-shaped flagpole finials (Oren, p. 160; Esin, p. 45 plate 9d).

Figs. 124–25   Shields with rope-like serpents (Seeck, *Oc.* V, 75, 96 [pp. 118–19]).

Fig. 126   Germanic brooch with stylized dragon (Kühn, p. 121 fig. 4).

Fig. 127   Han dynasty bronze TLV mirror (Bulling, p. XXIV plate 42).

Fig. 128   Han dynasty bronze mirror with interlocking brackets on knob (inset) (Bulling, p. 76).

Great Chain of Nothing: Buddhist Emptiness in Calvin's Mysticism

by Crerar Douglas

I do not know why the European Middle Ages ended. In fact, it is hard to know what it means to say they ended. What if there never were any Middle Ages anyway? Was that not just a name slapped onto the bulk of European history by bourgeois liberals who thought they were modern and wanted some term of opprobrium for people who were not?

If we were to seek a less prejudicial term for the Middle Ages, a most reasonable answer would be the Sacramental Ages. Whatever cultural disunity the Middle Ages experienced, they still had a unity unknown to us in their mandala of sacraments, a wheel with six spokes joined at the Eucharist in the middle. Luther, Calvin, and company did much to destroy that sacramental unity. They thought they were Reformers, and yet they were also destroyers. So, to say that the Middle Ages ended is really to say that the sacramental mandala lost its centrality in European culture.

Are there any parallels in religious history to this massive world-view destruction which lies at the origin of the Protestant-Catholic division of Western Christendom? One wonders about King Josiah's Deuteronomic Reform in ancient Israel or, on a vaster scale, Muhammad's Qur'anic Reformation-Destruction, both of them book-centered, iconoclastic, and violent like the European Reformation. One wonders whether Nichiren's Lotus Sutra revolution in Japan was moving in a similar direction.

It can be argued, of course, that the Reformation was not mainly about bookocentricity and iconoclasm, but rather the experience of the free outpouring of grace, a kind of flood of forgiveness bypassing the Church of Rome as if it were a Berlin Wall. In that case, the closest analogue might be the rise of the Pure Land School of Buddhism, when so many people became convinced that the source of their deliverance was not their own power but the gracious vow of the bodhisattva—the power of "the other."

If there is any similarity between the Reformation and the rise of the Pure Land School, one must ask whether the revolution that underlies all of Mahayana Buddhism, the Madhyamikan revolution of India, is even closer to the European Reformation, at least conceptually, although not politically. The Madhyamikan revolution, wrought above all by Nagarjuna and Candrakirti, was the dismantling of a whole culture's sacramental stability. The Madhyamikans were undermining India's ancient hierarchy of grace, its cosmic plenitudes, and its great chain of being, by destroying the very concept of essence.

The purpose of this paper is to speculate about possible similarities between Madhyamika Buddhism and John Calvin's Christianity. My approach, following Hans-Georg Gadamer's dictum that truth eludes the methodical person, will be self-consciously careless and, I hope, wide-ranging.

Furthermore, I am taking the methodologically suicidal path of ignoring primary sources. Instead of discussing the texts of the Madhyamikans and the Reformers themselves, I am going to seek inspiration (quite unearned and unmerited by me) in the free grace of two dazzling scholars who know much more about the primary sources than I do: Gadjin Nagao, Professor Emeritus of Buddhist Studies at Kyoto University and member of the Kyoto School of Pure Land Buddhism, and Thomas F. Torrance, Professor Emeritus of Christian Dogmatics at the University of Edinburgh and former Moderator of the Church of Scotland.

I first learned about Nagao from my California State University, Northridge (CSUN) colleague Mokusen Miyuki and about Torrance from another CSUN colleague, Robert D. Shofner. Certainly Miyuki and Shofner deserve no blame for what follows, but I want to record my gratitude to them for starting me down a path of which they may or may not approve.

Now on with it! I shall jump onto the backs of Nagao and Torrance, treating them as racehorses who will gallop me through meadows of Buddha-land and Calvin-land that I could not begin to walk through on my own. No primary sources. No proofs. Just speculation.

Both Nagao and Torrance are especially concerned to show how a proper understanding of their respective religious traditions can help the world, especially the Western world, overcome its epidemic addiction to dualism, that habit of mind by which we divide everything into mutually contradictory opposites: subject and object, mind and body, mind and matter, self and ecology, self and humanity, God and devil, left and right, black and white, man and woman, straight and gay, Communist and innocent, the good guys and the bad guys. At the same time, Nagao and Torrance are equally concerned to refute the monism by which we often attempt to escape from dualism, because monism imprisons the self in itself.

Still, if dualism and monism are both unsatisfactory, a Hegelian dialectic of monism and nihilism is no more helpful, even if more interesting. According to Nagao and Torrance, the dialectic cannot save us because, like dualism, monism, nihilism, and pluralism, dialectic is still a completely this-worldly philosophy. The self is still not out of prison.

Here we must cry "Whoa!" for an instant, to note how weird it sounds to modern ears that there are modern people who seriously consider themselves honest intellectuals and yet claim that they rationally believe that this world is not all there is. It sounds un-American, and, thank God, it is!

Nagao believes that awakening yields a true insight into this world that is totally contrary to the conventional reasoning of this world (even though the true insight turns out also to be identical to the world of conventional reasoning, but more of that in a moment). And Torrance believes that God in Christ has given us a revelation of truth that is totally contrary to the conventional reasoning of this world (even though in his revelation God has identified himself completely with the world of conventional reasoning).

Just as the chasm between Torrance's Calvinist God and Nagao's Buddhist emptiness is unbridgeable, so is the chasm between enlightenment and revelation unbridgeable. The traditions are as distinct from each other as different planets. The chasm is indeed unbridgeable, although I might say that with God all things are possible, and the Buddhist would add that enlightenment always takes us by surprise. Still, that was then; this is now. Buddhism is Buddhism; Christianity is Christianity, and never the twain shall meet. Conceptually, that is. But in daily life, of course, we eat each other's food, marry each other, have babies, live and die and play together, whether emptiness is emptiness or God is God. Conceptually, the difference between a Nagarjuna and a Calvin is as undeniable as the difference between a Nagao and a Torrance. But the similarity is equally important.

The heart of the similarity between Nagao and Torrance lies in their critical-realist epistemologies; Nagao and Torrance make no distinction between noumena and phenomena. In knowing reality we know reality, not just its appearances. But their realism is critical inasmuch as they stress the limitations of our knowledge, limitations caused both by the finitude of our standpoint and by the inadequacies of our powers of vision, even after that vision has been enlarged by what Nagao calls awakening and Torrance calls divine revelation.

Different as enlightenment and revelation are, then, they are nevertheless similar in their effect on Nagao's and Torrance's epistemologies: both think that this reality that is absolutely other does not remove us from the ordinary world in its finitude but opens our eyes to it, precisely in its ordinariness and finitude, for the first time in our lives. Awakening and revelation give us no rocket out of the ordinary or primrose path around it but a royal road to the heart of the ordinary, a road which has itself been ordinary, with all our errors and imitations still dogging us so rudely.

Enlightenment and revelation may or may not zap us. If they do, they enter us, turn the lights on inside and outside, transfigure us. They are ours. But they are not ours in the sense of being domesticatable. Enlightenment and revelation roar like a lion. If they do not scare the hell out of you, you do not know anything about them. They are truly other.

For Nagao, the other is that truth which, and in which, the awakened person sees. The awakened one sees that the willows are green and the flowers red, but of course the unawakened one also sees that. Only the awakened one can understand the difference, and the similarity, between the two visions. Yet Nagao argues that, for Nagarjuna and Candrakirti, the silence which the awakened one has discovered does not preclude speech. On the contrary, the Buddha did not use his enlightenment to propel himself out of the world of conventional understanding. Instead, the Buddha expressed in the world of conventional understanding that very truth which is its opposite. This was compassionate. It was a compassion totally other than the way of ordinary understanding, and yet totally identified with it, because such identification is the path of the enlightened one. Compassionate enlightenment, just as it is other-derived, must be other-directed.

What the awakened one sees is that the true insight bestowed by enlightenment is identical with that conventional, worldly understanding which is its total opposite. The two truths are identical, however, not as a result of anything natural or essential, since true insight sees what conventional insight cannot see—that there are not natures or essences. So the two truths are identical not by nature but by the opposite of nature, by true insight. It is the other that grounds what we ordinarily perceive as not-other. But when we perceive that the not-other is grounded by the other, we perceive that the other is not other; that the not-other is other; and that there is no ground.

What true insight sees when it sees the willows are green and the flowers red, is that the dependent co-arising which is the willows and the flowers is in fact emptiness. This does not mean that the willows and flowers are unreal, illusory, or in any sense ultimately nothing. Being nothing is only half (as it were) of emptiness. The other half is nothing in the act of being. Hence insight into the emptiness of dependent co-arising is not, for the Madhyamika philosopher, a world-denying ascetic nihilism of some kind.

Nor is the awakened person's vision of the greenness of the willows and the redness of the flowers a product of some kind of inspiration, whether divine or artistic. True insight may produce artistic inspiration or aid in scientific discovery. Or it may not. In either case, the insight into the truth is not the product of inspiration, art, genius, science, or discussion. It is totally other. Awakening can be represented by the descent of the bodhisattva from the world of true insight into the world of conventional reasoning. Awakening is the descent of nirvana into samsara, except that nirvana and samsara were always at the same time opposite and identical. Awakening is the gracious re-engagement of the one who is freed from all engagement. It is entirely other-power, not own-power. It is entirely without essences, either our essence or the other's essence, because true insight sees that there are no essences in spite of the fact that conventional reasoning thinks there are, but, since it has seen the identity of true insight and conventional understanding, true insight can (compassionately) speak the language of conventional understanding with its supposed essences and natures: the conventional is not false in its own realm but true as far as it goes, i.e., not all the way to ultimacy.

True insight sees that all is without essence, that everything is what it is, not on its own, but interdependently. Everything dependently co-arises. Everything *is* by ceaselessly interacting with everything else, deriving its very being not from itself but from its interaction with others, in such a way that the words "thing," "being," and "others" coalesce, or—Calvin would say— are as if in a covenant with one another. True insight sees that the interaction by which the willows are green and flowers red is ceaseless and yet is also the story of ceasing. The willows will not always be green. They are such now. The ceasing is ceaseless. There can be no static nature or framework of natures, no great chain of being, because the chain is one of ceaselessly ceasing dependent co-arising.

The opposite worlds of conventional understanding and true insight, then, are identical only because, as it were, the path of the bodhisattva's descent bridges the gap between the two truths, but the path of ascent does not bridge the gap, except in retrospect. Only in retrospect can the bodhisattva who has ascended to true insight look back on the path of ascent that had been followed and see that it was after all the traditional bodhisattva path of ascent. But by that time the bodhisattva has descended again, so that, in every way, only the descent makes possible the ascent. Everything is other-power, compassion, not own-power; skillful ascent only because of gracious descent. But both the ascent and the descent are "real," critically real.

It is important to recognize that the bodhisattva does not wear rose-colored glasses. The bodhisattva is not an idealist. When the bodhisattva descends from true insight to the realm of conventional understanding, it is in no sense for sentimental or deluded reasons. The bodhisattva is a critical realist, seeing the conventional world as the dangerous, beautiful, and suffering-plagued place that it really is. The bodhisattva sees through the delusions of conventional understanding because the bodhisattva sees from a perspective that is totally other than the conventional.

The idealist absolute, for instance Hegel's, is the essence of our conventional world. The bodhisattva's realist absolute is the opposite of our conventional world. The idealist absolute loses its self-consciousness in its identity with the world. The realist absolute retains its self-consciousness throughout its compassionate identification with the world. The idealist absolute must by definition be the essence of the world. The bodhisattva's realist absolute, which after all *is* the bodhisattva, must not be any thing by definition. In the freedom of total otherness the realist absolute identifies with that of which it is the complete opposite. That is compassion, not essentialism; true freedom, not determinism.

Nagao's realist absolute is so other than our world that, like Calvin's, Barth's, and Torrance's, it cannot even be adequately described by the phrase "wholly other" because that phrase itself becomes a static essence, thereby domesticating and falsifying the otherness of the other, and to that extent making it our creation or our projection and ultimately, therefore, our own essence. No salvation there. No deliverance. Our hope is only in the truly other. Nagao's other, like Torrance's Jesus, loves me only because that other chooses to love me. This I know, for the Bible and the Lotus Sutra tell me so. Other-power, not in any sense whatever own-power. There it is: Calvinism pure and simple! Fire-eating, bagpipe Calvinism. The heather is purple, and the haggis delicious.

The structural similarity, then, between the epistemologies of Nagao and Torrance is that for both something totally other, conventional understanding relativizes that understanding without destroying it, attacking it, or merging with it. Hence there is no dialectic between conventional truth and true insight because conventional truth has no claims on true insight. Their total otherness to each other frees them from each other. True insight is entirely superior to conventional understanding, in no sense its product or necessary counterpart. The provisional truth of our conventional world is (when seen from the perspective of true insight) made possible only by the ultimate truth of the world of awakening. The conventional world is free by itself but infinitely freer when bound to that which absolutely, graciously, and salvifically binds itself to it.

Hence, for both Nagao and Torrance, the reality which allows us to be realists is not our reality but the opposite of our reality binding itself to our reality, and the total otherness of that which allows us to be realists requires us to be critical realists. Hence idealism, monism, dualism, dialectic, and nihilism are all banished. The Madhyamikan standpoint, like the standpoints of Calvin, Barth, and Torrance, is the standpoint of no standpoint—the standpoint that is always other and therefore always compassionately close to us. For both Nagao and Torrance, only in compassion can the absolutely other bind itself to us, and, for both, that compassionate other is the ground (while infinitely transcending ground) of our reality.

At the heart of Torrance's Calvinism is his belief that from the century after St. Athanasius, Christianity has embroiled itself in philosophical standpoints that betray it. These false standpoints are the same falsehoods we have seen Nagao attacking: dualism (the root of them all), monism, idealism, dialectic, nihilism, all of them static standpoints that, for Torrance, exclude a transcendent God from our consciousness in very much the same way as Nagao thinks they exclude true insight from conventional understanding. Yet, for both, reality will triumph, because it already has.

Torrance is very sweeping (some think absurd) in his indictment of Christian dualism. According to Torrance, the early Christian effort to translate the gospel into Greek by transforming Greek categories from static to dynamic collapsed during the century after Athanasius. The result was that the Greek dualist categories of stasis and essence snuffed out the gospel, or almost snuffed it out. During the Reformation, a few Reformers (notably our hero St. Calvin) began to rescue the gospel from the clutches of the dualist categories, but during the seventeenth century the renewed Aristotelianism of the scholastics, both Protestant and Catholic, snuffed out the gospel again, or almost, and at the hands of Newton the gospel took one of its worst drubbings because the universe became a closed box from which God was effectively excluded—contrary to Newton's intention—except for emergency repairs and unnatural acts.

Kant thought he was rescuing the gospel by re-installing it in the world of space and time, safe and sound in the organic and romantic hollows of the mind of the observer, but the hollows turned out to be as dualist as Newton's nature, because the observer, having excluded God from the kingdom of fact, made him jump rope obediently all alone in the kindergarten of value.

Who would you guess finally rode in on a white horse to rescue the gospel? None other than St. Albert Einstein of Princeton. The end. Everyone started wearing orange and black again, and the Church of Scotland lived happily ever after.

I do not wish to claim that Torrance is so flippant about his *Heilsgeschichte* as this crude summary would suggest, only that he would perhaps be more bearable if he were more flippant once in a while. It is all so ludicrous and itself so dualist at first sight: Pope Leo the Great, the Cappadocian Fathers,

Augustine, Aquinas, Luther, Newton, Kant, Hegel, and Bultmann as evil knights; St. Athanasius, Richard of St. Victor, Grosseteste and Pseudo-Grosseteste, James Clerk Maxwell and Michael Faraday, Einstein, Michael Polanyi, and Sir Torrance in the army of God and King Arthur!

But there is more. Every dualist narrative has one culprit who is the very epitome of evil. Who is the Darth Vader of Torrance's thriller? In good Calvinist fashion the culprit is not a person at all but an abstraction. Torrance's culprit is the receptacle-concept of space.

Why? For starters, because it is false cosmology, because Sir Albert proved it false. But, we might ask, are Augustine, Aquinas, Luther, Newton, and company to be held accountable for knowing something that was not discovered until the twentieth century? To a certain extent, yes. Because Athanasius, Cyril of Alexandria, John Philoponus of Alexandria, and Hilary of Poitiers, among others, having already seen the limitations of the receptacle-concept of space, had actually begun to replace it with non-dualist models that turned out to be closer to the space-time continuum than to the static receptacle-model. But the church, both East and West, neglected, distorted, and often attempted to destroy these efforts in favor of dualist conceptions derived from Greek philosophy. It was as if the church wanted to escape from the dangerous, open-ended, dynamic universe set forth in the gospel, a universe in which space is not static but time-driven, not permanent, but created by God out of nothing, not resting undisturbed in its silence, but called forward by a dynamic that extends from an origin in time to a culmination in time.

The church, says Torrance, preferred to think of itself as living in a static receptacle from which human logic could build a bridge toward a God who was conceived not as in motion but unmoved, not a first and foremost interdependently Trinitarian (and therefore, in Nagao's sense, co-arising), but first and foremost statically one and only by special revelation—almost as an after-thought—"known" to be Trinitarian. The church was trying to blend own-power and other-power, building a stepladder of ontological, cosmological, teleological, and anthropological argument for the "existence" of a static God and finding truly nothing (but afraid to call it that), no one at the top of the ladder but the human self who had built the ladder and ascended it. The church was trying (in Nagao's Buddhist words) to construct true insight from conventional understanding, and it cannot be done.

So many things are offensive at first in Torrance's narrative. One hardly knows where to begin in criticizing it. But skipping over disputes about particular cases of historical unfairness, one wants to cry out at once against the Calvinist totalitarianism of it, the mixing of categories which Kant taught us to keep separate: fact and value, science and religion, cosmology and morality. How can Torrance be so un-Kantian as to claim that to the extent that Christianity has been based on a false cosmology for fifteen centuries it has been false? How can one's cosmology invalidate one's religion? Is not religious invalidation solely the privilege of one's moral turpitude and aesthetic *gaucherie?*

As a critical realist, however, Torrance wants to follow Einstein and Michael Polanyi in attempting to undo the Kantian distinction between fact and value. If he succeeds, the other nice walls tumble down too—between science and religion, between cosmology and morality. In this project, Torrance develops a natural theology which is the opposite of traditional Christian natural theology. Torrance's natural theology is, following Barth's, not prior to the theology of the Word of God but subordinate to it. He compares this shift to Einstein's shifting of geometry from its independent Euclidean status to its Einsteinian status, subordinate to natural science. This shift parallels, it seems to me, Nagao's placement of the path to awakening not logically prior to awakening but subordinate to it. In good Barthian fashion, dare we say, Torrance, Einstein, and Nagao establish the reality first and the possibility only afterward.

Torrance's eschatologically organized universe, temporary thing that it is, is like Calvin's cathedral, or emptied-out cathedral. Word has dynamized out icon; time has crashed in on place, movement on stasis, eschatology on ecclesiology. The place is an organism, not a container, a community, not a box. The place is (will you permit me to say it?) dependently co-arising with the people. In Calvin's "cathedral" does Christ become present through transubstantiation in the elements on the altar? No. The elements are containers, and the risen Christ is uncontainable. The static cannot contain the dynamic. Essence cannot be transformed because there are no essences.

Then is Christ really present in eucharistic worship? Indeed. Just spiritually, as for Zwingli, in our memories? Not so. Christ is really present in the Eucharist for Calvin, sacramentally present. Then because he is omnipresent in nature and in the Eucharist he becomes salvifically present? No. That is Luther. For Calvin, Christ is not physically omnipresent in nature. Luther's view still presupposes the container-concept of space, and it reduces the salvific presence of Christ to the vanishing-point of the timeless sacramental moment. Hence it is prototypical Hegelianism (Luther would shout *Nein!* to hear us saying this): a dialectic of monism and nihilism, *iustificatio* and *Anfechtung*. Then is Christ present in the eucharistic action itself? in the ritual? No, that is Melanchthon. For Calvin that kind of presence is not real enough, (perhaps surprisingly) not physical enough.

Then where is Christ physically present? For Calvin, as for Karlstadt (that cad), we cannot talk about Christ's physical presence without speaking critical-realistically about his space-time presence. The space-time continuum-concept is at work in what Calvin's critics called his *extra Calvinisticum,* dynamizing out the receptacle idea: Karlstadt and Calvin are saying that Christ is spatially present only where he is temporally present. What is as sacred as Christ's presence is the mode of his absence: the fact that he has passed over to the eschaton and we have not. Hence, for Karlstadt and Calvin, Christ is present only where he is *at* present: at the top of heaven and the end of time. For Karlstadt, we reach him only spiritually, in Holy *Gelassenheit*, which Luther (rude man that he was) likened to swallowing the Holy Spirit feathers and all. But Calvin was not quite so easy to tag. For Calvin, Christ has left us his Karlstadtian holy absence, indeed, but he has also left us a very real sacramental presence. Spiritually, of course, Christ is both here and there, both in this world and in the other world, but physically only in the other world. For Calvin, our ordinary understanding of space and time must be mystically fractured by the Holy Spirit and recreated if we are really to partake of Christ. The Holy Spirit sursums your corda, truly—that is, mystically—lifting you into the other world in the Eucharist, where, indeed, you really partake of Christ.

The real presence, for Calvin, does not destroy the real absence or have a dialectic with it, just as, for Nagao, dependent co-arising does not destroy emptiness or merge into it. In Christ, the presence and absence are not at odds with each other: there and here, then and now, do *not* (T. S. Eliot to the contrary notwithstanding) "cease to matter." Rather they are (as Wallace Stevens more stubbornly would put it) reconciled. Here remains here. There remains there. The distinction remains, and it matters, but here and not-here are reconciled.

Who is not familiar with the experience of the divine absence? It is not the same as the experience of the divine presence. The difference matters. Calvin is asking in his own very sixteenth-century way whether, in the scheme of things, the divine absence is not just as important and sacred as the divine presence. They are not the same. But they are not each other's contrary either: the absence and the presence are each other's complement. As Stevens put it in "Peter Quince at the Clavier":

> Beauty is momentary in the mind—
> The fitful tracing of a portal;
> But in the flesh it is immortal.

Whatever Stevens may or may not have intended (which matters not a whit to a Gadamerian like me), he can be heard saying that there is no love without absence (as in the woman's wordless worship in "Sunday Morning"). Absence, since it is not the opposite of presence, is the holy opportunity of presence. In the beauty of love, flesh and immortality are not each other's opposite but each other's opportunity. The immortality of the flesh is not in the mind: it must be in the flesh, made new by that love of which beauty is the symbol.

Have we slipped a cog from Calvinism? Nay, Stevens called himself a "dried-up Presbyterian" with good reason (his jokes were always serious): he was downright Puritan—nay, Miltonic—in his mysticism of fleshly immortality, and if we think Calvin was unpoetic, we need to re-read his eucharistic writings, not just the polemical ones, but especially the passages in which the subject comes up in the commentaries: it is the poetry of immortal flesh.

If the divine absence was so important to Calvin, did he think it was because there had been some kind of slip-up in the universe; a little mistake of some kind had crept in without God's awareness or permission? Nay, we can bet our bottom dollar that Calvin's universe had no slip-ups. The experience of the divine absence is here for a reason.

For Calvin, Christ descended (like the bodhisattva, I would rashly say) to be with us in the flesh, but now in his immortal flesh he has ascended and gone on ahead of us to the place that he will show us. Christ called us out of nothing into being in the first place. He calls us now into more nothing, into more being, so that we will be infinitely other than, yet graciously identical to, the person we are now. Christ calls us to His resurrection.

When we are experiencing the absence of God, then, what we are experiencing is God's transcendence of our static categories. God refuses to let us nail him down again. Once was enough. He is risen. For Calvin, then, there is no static experience of God. Calvin's mystic space through which the Holy Spirit whirls you is closer to Milton's than to Dante's, not filled with grace because not filled with anything—empty—but energized by grace, more Einsteinian, in its defiance of our common-sense expectations, than Newtonian.

Not static but, as in a Mannerist painting, hurled beyond itself, Calvin's inner spiritual space is the emptiness of that dependent co-arising which the Holy One of Israel called the covenant and Rembrandt translated onto canvas, the covenant with venerable patriarchs and matriarchs (not necessarily in harmony with each other at all times but deriving their lives from each other), the covenant that is a reconciler of dualities—time and eternity, divinity and humanity, inwardness and outwardness, rich and needy, female and male, young and old—a covenant created out of nothing, spoken into existence by God's invisible Word in the darkness that shines like Rembrandt's candle just beyond the canvas.

So the end of humanity's dualist nightmare is where it started: in the Garden of Eden. Dualism ends in the Garden because the covenant begins there. The covenant reconciles without destroying. It brings together all the dualities that can be reconciled. And it is the means by which the dualities that cannot be reconciled (good versus evil and life versus death) have been resolved. Their negation has been negated. Sin and death now have only the power we choose to give them. In God's fulfillment of his own covenant, by taking the part of both the divine partner and the human partner, he destroyed sin and death, and he reconciled our mortality with his immortality, thereby bridging the universe's largest chasm, one we, not he, had caused. By fulfilling both the human and the divine sides of his own covenant, God made sure that, no matter what, his will be done.

Giordano Bruno was dizzied by the apparently formless emptiness to which the Renaissance was so reluctantly waking up. Pascal was frightened by it. Calvin, like Milton, gloried in it. In Calvin's emptiness we are not on firm ground. We are not essence. We dangle, like Jonathan Edwards' spider. We are other-dependent through and through. But so is everyone else, and that is why we take our nourishment from God's good covenant. We arise not independently but dependently, covenantally. In the Holy Spirit Calvin's Christians ascend and descend from world to world, and, like the bodhisattva (if I may be so bold), disengage only to re-engage, until their disengagement and their re-engagement in the world become one act, one prayer.

The haggis and the heather, the flowers and the willows, the Big Quake of the future and the Big Bang of the past: all of them are empty like us, dependently co-arising like us, with us, in us, and all around us, simultaneously, as it were, both synchronically and diachronically, and in that sense both free and predestined, both free and karmic, free only because predestined, free only because karmic. The only question is whether the "order" is gracious, and the only answer is yes. Calvin ended the Middle Ages by picking up the sacramental mandala and whirling it like a Frisbee toward the hand of God, who is infinitely far away and yet in the center of all our circumferences. So the Buddha spun the wheel of *dharma* into life and compassion.

Calvin's favorite image for the universe (in case you think all this mysticism is getting a tad melodramatic) was that the universe is like a theater, a theater of the glory of God. When the metaphysics and the essences, the human stepladders to God, have all been moved away, so that the scene can change for the last time, Calvin would have said, I am sure, unlike the theater-phobic Calvinists who betrayed their master, that in the power of God's love we can finally rejoice that things do not last forever as they are now—that we are such stuff as dreams are made of. Our emptiness is sacred. Calvin would then go on, I am sure, to quote with warm approval the view that we are "all spirits, and will melt into air, into thin air; and, like the baseless fabric of our vision, the cloud-capp'd towers, the gorgeous palaces, the solemn temples, the great globe itself, yea, all which it inherits, we shall dissolve and, like this insubstantial pageant faded, leave not a rack behind."

Rejoice! For only then will we see face to face that everything in the theater has all along been a revelation, a revelation of the glory of God, and then we will be ready to enjoy him forever. The Buddhist would not say that. But with God all things are possible. The Buddhist would not say that either. But, we recall, the Buddhist might very well say that enlightenment always takes us by surprise. Let the Buddhist have the last word!

I am quite aware that I may not be dealing with a real Buddhism or a real Calvinism at all, but rather with figments of my imagination. The very first bronc may have thrown me in the first minute of my fantasy, and the pain will not sink in until your responses show me that I have in fact for a long time been on the ground, sitting on what our national playwright, Peggy Noonan, would call my keester.

CALIFORNIA STATE UNIVERSITY, NORTHRIDGE

The Cookie *Computus*

by Barnabas B. Hughes, O. F. M.

Computi are of two kinds: ecclesiastical and vulgar. The former has for its purpose the determination of the Easter date; hence, it is necessary for the construction of the calendar. The work *De temporum ratione* by the Venerable Bede contains perhaps the clearest of the early explanations for fixing on which Sunday after March 21 Easter shall fall. Another work mistakenly attributed to Bede, *De computo vel loquela digitorum,* exemplifies the vulgar *computus.* It sets forth the rules or algorithms for ordinary arithmetic computations: addition, subtraction, multiplication, division, halving and doubling, squaring numbers and finding roots. Of the two meanings for the word *computus,* however, the ecclesiastical is more commonly understood.[1] There is, however, an interesting exception to both these functions of the *computus.*

A onetime empty column in a sheaf of calendric pages was filled, perhaps as early as 1401, with an unusual poem in Swiss-German. The sheaf is now bound in Codex F.V.15 in the University Library, Basel, Switzerland.[2] Sometime the property of the Carthusian Abbey in Basel, the codex contains astronomical and religious tracts, all save one written in Latin. This interesting exception in verse is on folio 15rb. The purpose of the poem is to set the date for making Easter cookies. Before offering a transcription of the text and a reproduction of the folio page (figure 1), a few remarks about the text are fitting.

The author addressed the poem to an unknown "dear friend" to whom he acknowledges his indebtedness for past favors and offers a small token in repayment. Apparently, his dear friend wished to know how to compute not only the Easter date but also *fasenacht,* the eve of Ash Wednesday. On this date, the author notes, "cookies are generally baked." In view of references to Christmas, the modern reader may assume that there were Easter cookies as well as *Weinachtskuchen* which had to be prepared well in advance of the feast. The Easter date, as the author makes clear, depends on discovering the Golden Number. Once this is known, it is a simple matter to count back to Lenten eve. To round out the picture, the author adds (in Latin and without breaking the series of rhyming couplets!) the *postscriptum* that once Easter has been found, then by counting backwards his good friend can fix the days

---

[1] The standard work on the *computus* is that of A. Cordoliani. Beginning in 1942 with "Etudes de comput," *Bibliothèque de l'Ecole des Chartres* 103: 61–68, he published some thirty-five articles on the *computus,* the last (to my knowledge) in 1961.

[2] I wish to acknowledge the courtesy of Dr. Max Burckhardt, director of the Manuscript Division, University Library, Basel, when I visited there in 1972. He pointed out to me that a number of the German words are still in use today among the Swiss who dwell in the mountains.

on which fall *quadragesima, quinquagesima, sexagesima* and *septuagesima*
Sundays.

The location of the poem in the calendar may not have been arbitrary.
Concerned with fixing the date for the inception of the Lenten season, the
author may quite deliberately have placed the poem beside the column of the
calendar which concludes March and begins April, for Easter generally falls
in this period of time. This suggests that the composition of the poem was
hardly an afterthought to fill space.

Arguing for the date of composition, unlike assigning authorship of the
poem, is comparatively easy. Folio 16r, which was written by the same hand as
the poem, carries the date 1401. Indeed, the reader can recognize the work of
the same scribe by comparing the script of the poem with the script of the
calendric column to its left.

Of codical interest are these items: The page is paper with the watermark S
(Briquet III, n. 9040). The text is written in brown ink, the initial capital in
red, and red strokes flow through the other brown capitals. The last three lines
(in Latin) are in red ink; the margins are ruled in brown. The pages measure
212.3 x 29.8 cm; the text area is 5.9 x 21.0 cm. The photocopied
reproduction (figure 1) is shown at about 70 percent of the original size. The
numbering of every fifth line is mine.

> Lieber freund mit dienstan hast mich
> Gebunden vast vnd vnsaglich
> darvm von mir solt sin gewert
> alles daz din hertz begert
> als vil ich mag ietz vnd och hienach   5
> sussz an dem minstem ich an vach
> du woltest gern wen ich fuer war
> weleg tags kem in dem iar
> der ostertag vnd dar zu
> die vasnach spat vnd och fru   10
> des bewis ich dich gar kurtzlich
> da by du es weist sicherlich
> der guldin zal nim eben war
> welha die sig in dem iar
> da wiss wilt du den ostertag   15
> wenn du sy hie vindest ich dir sag
> daz der naechst sunnentag
> ist an vaell der ostertag
> Kaem aber die zal davor genant
> vff dem sunnentag so sig erkant   20
> dir lieber gesell die lere och
> das denn der trag nit singet noch
> Resurrexi der nechst dar nach
> hat denn daz ampt daz man anvach
> denn ze singen als ich redd .E.   25

Noch denn sag ich dir me
die linien da der ostertag
Inne kumpt ich dir daz sag
Nu an wenken die richci hin
Ze rechter hand schrib ich dir in   30
die zal der wochen vnd der tag
die wir hant von dem heiligen tag
Ze wisnacht vnd der vasenacht
So man gemeinlich kuechli bacht
Alsussz hast du daz wol bericht   35
Gen got bit ich vergiss min nicht
Invento autem pasca computando modo
retrogrado faciliter inveniri po
terit . xl . l . lx . et lxx.

CALIFORNIA STATE UNIVERSITY, NORTHRIDGE

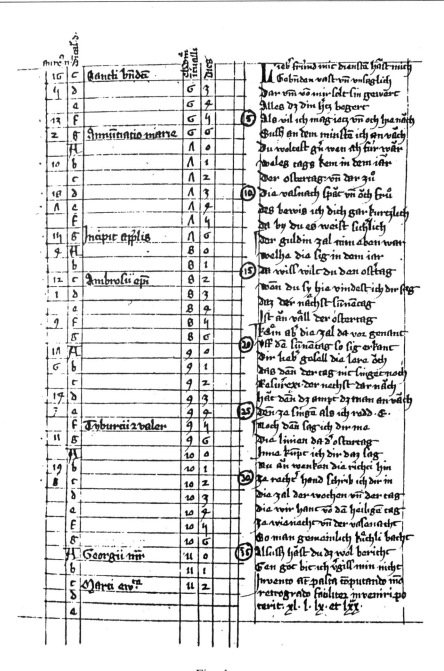

Fig. 1.

The Role of Alfred of Sareshel in the Dissemination of Eastern Medical Learning in the Latin West

by James K. Otte

Alfred of Sareshel was a twelfth-century English scholar who went to Spain in order to translate Greek and Arabic natural philosophy into Latin.[1] He also wrote several commentaries on Greek and Arabic works,[2] and he was the first Latin commentator on Aristotle since the time of Boethius (d. 524). Moreover, Alfred wrote an independent treatise on the movement of the heart, the *De motu cordis*.[3]

This medical treatise, and his frequent discussions of and allusions to medical topics in his commentary on Aristotle's *Metheora,* demonstrate Alfred's extensive knowledge and profound interest in medicine. In my recent edition of *Alfred of Sareshel's Commentary on the* Metheora *of Aristotle*, I therefore posited the question whether Alfred might have been a *professor medicine*.[4] Then, in a paper presented at the meeting of the Medieval Academy of the Pacific at UCLA in April 1989, I explored that topic in some detail by summarizing the evidence that led me to such a hypothesis. And I am continuing my investigation.

Whatever that search may yield, it is evident already that Alfred occupies a major position in the dissemination of Eastern medical knowledge in the Latin West. He cites an impressive number of Greek, Arabic, and Jewish medical authors. Among others, Alfred quotes from Hippocrates, Galen, Honain ibn Ishak, Avicenna, Costa ben Luca, and Isaac Israeli.[5] Further, the number of Aristotelian references in Alfred's works is unequaled by any other writer of his time.[6]

This paper will seek to explain the traditions and versions of Alfred's medical sources. Further, it will demonstrate how Alfred used these authors.

He seems to have completed his last *opus*, the *De motu cordis*, around the year 1210,[7] and since he was a pioneer in the reception and dissemination of the "new

---

[1] J. K. Otte, *Alfred of Sareshel's Commentary on the* Metheora *of Aristotle* (Leiden, 1988), pp. 11–13.

[2] Ibid., pp. 13–15; R. J. Long, "Alfred of Sareshel's Commentary on the Pseudo-Aristotelian *De Plantis*: A Critical Edition," *Mediaeval Studies* XLVII, 125–67.

[3] C. Baeumker, *Die Stellung des Alfred von Sareshel (Alfredus Anglicus) und seiner Schrift De motu cordis in der Wissenschaft des beginnenden XIII. Jahrhunerts,* Sitzungsberichte der Königlich-Bayerischen Akademie der Wissenschaften IX (München, 1913); Baeumker, ed., *Des Alfred von Sareshel (Alfredus Anglicus) Schrift De motu cordis,* Beiträge zur Geschichte der Philosophie des Mittelalters XXIII (Münster, 1923).

[4] Otte, *Metheora,* p. 76.

[5] Baeumker, *De motu cordis,* pp. 97–98.

[6] Baeumker, *Stellung des Alfred,* p. 33: " . . . die grosse Zahl Aristotelischer Schriften, die in der *De motu cordis* angezogen sind, eine Häufung, die im Anfang des 13. Jahrhunderts nirgendwo sich finde."

[7] Otte, *Metheora,* pp. 4–6, 17–21; Baeumker, *Stellung des Alfred,* p. 48; cf. Baeumker, *De motu cordis,* p. vii n. 4, where he preferred a date closer to the year 1210; Long, *De plantis,* pp. 125–28.

learning," his commentaries and his *De motu cordis* provide a convenient and accurate gauge by which we can establish the extent and the quality of eastern medical knowledge in the Latin West around the year 1200.

Eastern medical science reached the Latin West in three phases, and in three different forms. First, there was the acquisition of the Greek medical corpus by the Romans. Only partially translated into Latin, and even further reduced by Roman encyclopedists, these handbooks provided the initial channel through which the early Middle Ages acquired its knowledge of Greek science in general, and its medical wisdom in particular. Secondly, there was the corpus of Greek medical treatises translated into Latin by a group of physicians in Ravenna between the fifth and the seventh centuries.[8] Thirdly, there were the translations of Greek and Arabic medical texts initiated by Constantine the African in the second half of the eleventh century, and completed during the Renaissance.

Medical knowledge in the early Middle Ages, therefore, was reduced to its limited inheritance from Rome, and to the translations made in Ravenna. Alfred belongs to the third phase. In it he played the dual role of translator and expositor. His commentaries were quoted frequently, and they enjoyed a wide geographic distribution. Moreover, his *De motu cordis* was used as a philosophical text by the Arts Faculty of Paris as early as the first half of the thirteenth century.[9]

But our knowledge of Alfred's life is still very incomplete, and most of our biographical information is based on hints in his writings. He dedicated his translation of the *De plantis* to Roger of Hereford[10] for whom we have two dates, 1176 and 1178.[11] Likewise, Alfred dedicated his *De motu cordis* to Alexander Neckham[12] who died in 1217.[13] Since the *De motu cordis* was Alfred's final work,[14] we can place his career in the closing decades of the twelfth and the early decades of the thirteenth centuries.

That Alfred was an Englishman is evident from a number of sources which refer to him as *Alfredus Anglicus*,[15] adding sometimes the geographic specification "Sarulensis" or "de Sarntehill," protean forms of the name for the English village Sareshel.[16] From *Anglicus* we can, in turn, deduce that Alfred

---

[8] D. C. Lindberg, ed., *Science in the Middle Ages* (Chicago, 1978), p. 54, and chapter 12, "Medicine," by Charles H. Talbot, who says, "But the main link in the transmission of ancient medical thought to the Middle Ages was the translation, made by Caelius Aurelianus in the fifth century, of the work of Soranus of Ephesus on acute and chronic diseases," p. 393.

[9] M. Grabmann, *Mittelalterliches Geistesleben,* 3 vols. (Hildesheim, 1926–56), II:192.

[10] Nicolai Damasceni, *De plantis libri duo Aristoteli vulgo adscripti,* ed. E. H. F. Meyer (Leipzig, 1841), p. 3 n. 1.

[11] C. H. Haskins, *Studies in the History of Mediaeval Science,* 2nd ed. (Cambridge, 1927), pp. 128–29. In his *Computus* for 1176 Roger referred to himself as *"iuvenis,"* while two years later he compiled an astronomical table for Hereford.

[12] Baeumker, *De motu cordis,* p. 1.

[13] T. Wright, ed., *Alexandri Neckam De naturis rerum libri duo* (London, 1863), p. XII.

[14] Otte, *Metheora,* pp. 17–21.

[15] Ibid., p. 9.

[16] S. D. Wingate, *The Mediaeval Latin Versions of the Aristotelian Scientific Corpus, with Special Reference to the Biological Works* (London, 1931), pp. 98–99 nn. 7, 10.

lived—at least for a time—in a place other than England. His teacher was a certain Salomon Avenraza (the name is probably the Latin form of ibn Ezra). Alfred calls him a "most celebrated Jew and preeminent modern philosopher,"[17] but who, in spite of Alfred's superlatives, remains unidentified. Alfred translated the *De plantis* and the *De congelatione et conglutinatione lapidum* from Arabic into Latin.[18] To accomplish that task, there was no better place than Spain, which the Arabs had initially conquered in 711. Spain also offered an environment where a Jewish scholar, Alfred's teacher, might thrive. Moreover, there are a number of Castilianisms in Alfred's vocabulary which clearly vouch for his *iter hispanicum*.[19] Alfred is also listed by Roger Bacon with several other translators,[20] and finally, he appears as a witness in a charter of c. 1220 as "Magister Alueredus de Sarutehill canonicus Lich."[21]

Let us now turn to an examination of Alfred's eastern medical sources, Greek, Arabic, and Jewish. The number of these sources increased with Alfred's maturity as a scholar, as he progressed from his commentaries on the *De plantis* to the *Metheora*, and concluded with his treatise on the movement of the heart, the *De motu cordis*.

Alfred's commentary on the *De plantis* was recently edited by R. James Long, who described its format as follows:

> Taking the form of a gloss, extending at times for a paragraph or more, on sixty-two words or phrases drawn from the first four chapters of the first book of the treatise and the final ten chapters of the second and last book, the commentary is notably shorter than the treatise commented upon.[22]

Short, also, is the list of eastern sources; the *De plantis* commentary is indeed devoid of any medical authors. Alfred borrowed a term from Avicenna whose *De congelatione et conglutinatione lapidum* he had translated.[23] But apparently he was not yet acquainted with the medical works of Avicenna, in whom Baeumker

---

[17] ". . . magister meus Salomon Avenraza, et Israelita celiberrimus, et modernorum philosophorum precipuus . . ." Otte, *Metheora,* p. 50:22–24.

[18] Avicennae, *De congelatione et conglutinatione lapidum,* being sections of the *Kitab al-Shifa,* ed. E. J. Holmyard and D. C. Mandeville (Paris, 1927).

[19] In his translation of the *De plantis* he uses the Spanish word *beleño* (latinized: *belenum*) to render the Arabic term for "henbane" or "nightshade" *(Hyoscyamus niger).* Otte, *Metheora,* p. 8 and n. 35. Cf. Long, *De plantis,* p. 126. In the translation of the *De congelatione et conglutinatione* he employs the Spanish word *arrova* (latinized: *arovarum*) to translate the Arabic term for a unit of weight. Otte, *Metheora,* p. 8 n. 36.

[20] J. S. Brewer, ed., *Fr. Rogeri Bacon: Opera Quaedam Hactenus Inedita* 3 (London, 1859), 471.

[21] J. C. Russell, *Dictionary of Writers of Thirteenth Century England* (London, 1936), p. 19.

[22] R. J. Long, "Alfred of Sareshel's Commentary on the Pseudo-Aristotelian *De plantis:* A Critical Edition," *Mediaeval Studies* XLVII (1985), 123.

[23] Long, *De plantis,* p. 131: "By the *congelata* [Alfred] means a whole class of metallic and non-metallic compounds which are formed by solidification." Cf. Haskins, *Studies in Mediaeval Science,* p. 94.

sees one of Alfred's "determining sources."[24]

By the time Alfred composed his commentary on the *Metheora*, his knowledge of the natural philosophy of Aristotle had considerably broadened. Moreover, his interests in medical topics had been established, particularly if we remember that the *Metheora* is, after all, a treatise whose first three books are devoted to meteorology, while book IV is concerned with chemistry. The commentary covers all four books of the *Metheora*. But while Alfred's glosses, comments, and commentaries vary considerably in length, his emphasis lay clearly with book IV, which received about 50 percent of his explanations. Here Alfred commented on no fewer than 123 *lemmata*. And while book IV is close to what we now call chemistry, Alfred used about one-fourth of its *lemmata* to indulge in medical discussions. Let us, therefore, examine his frequent references, allusions, and analogies to medicine.

Explaining the continuous heat of certain white-hot bodies in the interiors of the earth, he draws the analogy to pepper, ginger, and other spices which, when ingested, do not lose their inherent heat.[25] To Aristotle's discussion of the effect of heat and cold on homogeneous *(unigena)* and non-homogeneous *(non-unigena)* things, Alfred adds a more specific analysis by Alexander of Aphrodisias and then lists flesh and bone, besides gold and silver, as examples of homogeneous, and a hand or a foot, besides alloys composed of gold, silver, and copper, as examples of non-homogeneous items (53:3). Aristotle maintains that even though the primary substance, as well as the celestial bodies, have no physical contact with the lower regions, the former, nonetheless, influence the latter. Alfred again finds an analogy, likening their relationship to "the mysterious motion of certain properties, such as a magnet attracting iron, or scammonies attracting yellow bile *(cholor)* . . . whose cause is not evident" (39:16). In Medieval herbalogy, the resin from the roots of scammonies had medicinal application as a purgative.

A considerable portion of Alfred's discussion is devoted to *concoction* (i.e., the process in which various ingredients are combined), which he calls digestion *(digestio),* but which is much more inclusive than our meaning of that term because it includes the transformation of one thing into another. But, to complicate matters, Alfred also uses *digestio* in our sense when he speaks of the conversion of food in the alimentary canal for assimilation into the system. By Alfred's own definition, "concoction *(digestio)* is the transformation of one thing into another, like food and drink into fluids *(humores),* fluids into limbs" (59:48). Roasting by nature is concoction by dry heat, and he likens it to some humors causing melancholy (64:88). As other examples of inconcoction Alfred mentions the inability to change nourishment into humors and then into limbs, or when the discharge *(eductio)* is not suitable (60:59). With this passage we leave Alfred's generic definition of concoction and enter upon his explanations of the more specific concept of digestion.

---

[24] Baeumker, *Stellung des Alfred,* p. 63.

[25] Otte, *Metheora,* 47:2. All subsequent references to my edition of *Alfred of Sareshel's Commentary on the* Metheora *of Aristotle* are given in parentheses in which the first number refers to the page and the second number to the *lemma*.

Alfred follows Aristotle in pointing out that external aids (Aristotle mentions baths, Alexander of Aphrodisias includes exercises)[26] may aid natural heat in the process of digestion *(digestio),* but he adds, "natural heat is the principle of its digestion" (59:52). This theory is reminiscent of the famous experiment conducted by Frederick II of Hohenstaufen when he had two individuals disemboweled to determine the respective effects of rest and exercise upon digestion. Alfred then discusses two forms of nutrition. He says that in contrary nutrition, food and drink (in which there are many dissimilar nutrients) are assimilated. But humors are called similar nutrition since they have many similarities with what they nourish (59:52). Once again, Alfred assures us that it is heat which induces and attracts humor for the nutriment of things (57:34).

Alfred then points out that Aristotle set down signs by which one recognizes from a body's discharges *(superfluitates)* whether nourishment has undergone digestion or indigestion (60:56). Also, he adds that nourishment is facilitated by hot and more subtle humor and will result in its becoming lighter. And since watery parts are consumed more quickly into nourishment, the remainder becomes dry. He continues, "a doctor *(phisicus)* discovers in the bodily discharges excess of heat, dominance of dryness, abounding cold, or immoderate moisture, and other defects of nature" (60:58). More specifically, he maintains that digestion is greater when it proceeds naturally (60:60). Alfred offers a remedy for constipation when he advises, "digested things must sometimes be made more liquid, lighter, and looser by heat," and one for diarrhea when he cautions, "too much intemperance of heat, with the superfluous excess of moisture, results in immoderate density" (60:60). He then refers to several medical treatises, a *De urina* and a *Pronostica,*[27] and similar books, "which furnish a guide indicating whether the body is kept in proper balance with the content of the elementary qualities themselves." He concludes that doctors *(medici)* agree on the noted symptoms (60:58).

In the *Metheora* Aristotle condenses his entire theory of spontaneous generation into one sentence. He states, "Living things are generated in decaying matter because the natural heat which is expelled compounds them out of the material thrown off with it" (379b6). Accepting the theory, as one might expect him to, Alfred explains the process (58:42). But in another place, Alfred returns to that theme, maintaining that "certain animals are generated in the interiors of the body from decaying watery fluids *(flegmate putrefacto)* which are sometimes thrown up by vomiting" (65:89). He adds that some people assert that such animals are procreated in the stomach, which Aristotle refutes when he says, *"et*

---

[26] *Meteorologica* (379b24); cf. A. J. Smet, ed., *Alexandre d'Aphrodisias: Commentaire sur les météores d'Aristote* (Louvain, 1966), pp. 35–36.

[27] Otte, *Metheora,* p. 28, Latin text, 60:58; the reference is too general to allow positive identification of the authors. But the *Ars medicinae* contains treatises by these titles: *De urina* by Theophilus, and *Pronostica* by Hippocrates. Cf. A. Birkenmajer, "Le rôle joué par les médecins et les naturalistes dans la réception d'Aristote au XII-e et XIII-e siècles," *La Pologne au còngres international d'Oslo,* 1928 (Varsovie, 1930), pp. 4–5. Birkenmajer says, ". . . l'*Ars medicinae,* se composant de six brefs traités, à savoir: l' *Isagoge* de Johannitius, les *Aphorismes* et les *Pronostics* d'Hippocrate, les *Urinae* de Théophile, les *Pulsus* de Philarète et l'*Ars parva (Tegni)* de Galien."

animal non creatur in digestione" (65:90). Again, we must remember that *"digestio"* here means concoction, not digestion.

While Alfred's discussions above clearly demonstrate his interests in medicine, and more specifically in what is now called physiology, allow me to cite an example more akin to anatomy. Alfred maintains that the stomach is the place of digestion, and that in the stomach neither corruption nor, therefore, putrefaction takes place. He maintains that heat, motion, and effervescence prevent decay in the stomach. The "boiling" *(epsesis)* properly completed, [the alimentary matter,] which by nature is agreeable to nutrition, is attracted by the liver, which conveys the less appropriate material to the lower area of the digestive system. Digestion is almost complete in the intestine. Alfred then mentions a place "which is called *orbum* or *mantica* and which receives only the sediments of food, which by the regimen of nature decay and turn into feces." It is here that animals are generated which at times ascend to the stomach. And so, those who had asserted that animals are generated in the stomach are refuted, according to Alfred. He concludes that food is digested in the upper and decayed in the lower region *(utero),* which are segregated (65:90).

Once again Alfred has ventured far beyond Aristotle in descriptive detail and seemingly in the understanding of the subject. Unfortunately he does not provide us with a source for his knowledge. Also, he introduces an interesting medical term: *"orbum"* or *"mantica,"* which receives only the sediments of food, which by the regimen of nature decay and turn into feces. *Orbum* or *mantica* means "knapsack," and the lowest section of the ascending colon, i.e., the *caecum,* is still colloquially referred to as "the pouch."[28]

Let us now turn to Alfred's own treatise, the *De motu cordis,* which seems to have been his final *opus*. To be sure, Aristotle was Alfred's guide as he ventured into the realm of physiology and anatomy. Alfred cites him some forty times,[29] which prompted Baeumker, the editor of the *De motu cordis,* to observe, "The number of Aristotelian citations by Alfred is unequaled by any writer of the early thirteenth century."[30] What is perhaps even more remarkable is the fact that most, perhaps all, of his citations from Aristotle are taken from Greco-Latin translations.[31]

---

28 C. Baeumker, *De motu cordis,* p. 58 n. 3, was apparently flabbergasted by Alfred's statement: "Ex quibus cum muliebri semine permixtis si forte fit animal, ad similitudinem fit eorum quae in orbe procreantur." Two of his MSS had correctly *orbo* as the ablative of *orbum* [see R. A. Latham, *Revised Medieval Latin Word-List* (London, 1965), p. 324], but Baeumker chose *orbe* as ablative of *orbis:* "die freie Welt," something like "space."

29 The most frequent citations are from the *De anima,* but Alfred also cites the *Metheora, De somno et vigilia, De expiratione et respiratione, De phisico audito, Metaphisica, Ethica Nicomachia* and *Phisica,* as well as the pseudo-Aristotelian *De plantis* and the *Liber de causis.*

30 Baeumker, *Stellung des Alfred,* p. 33.

31 Ibid., pp. 35–43; cf. Grabmann, *Forschungen über die lateinischen Aristotelesübersetzungen des XIII. Jahrhunderts,* Beiträge zur Geschichte der Philosophie des Mittelalters. Texte und Untersuchungen, Band XVII, Heft 5–6 (Münster, 1916), 25. These initial Greco-Latin translations whose early appearance L. Minio-Paluello was able to document and partially credit to the translating activities of James of Venice, antedate a number of Arabo-Latin versions of the same Aristotelian treatises. (See Minio-Palluello, "Henry Aristippe, Guillaume de Moerbeke et les

In the *De motu cordis* Alfred's previous style takes a new form. While his commentaries on the *De plantis* and the *Metheora* took their cues from the *lemmata* of the texts before him, in his treatise *De motu cordis,* Alfred develops his theses and then supports them with his sources. Not limited to an investigation of the movement of the heart, the *De motu cordis* allowed Alfred to indulge freely in the realm of medicine. Almost devoid of the traditional Latin handbooks,[32] the sources of the *De motu cordis,* instead, are drawn from the medical works of Greek, Arabic, and Jewish authors. Among these, Aristotle held the status of *philosophus sapiens,* but others too, as the text below will show, received lavish praise, and Alfred cited them frequently.

But Alfred could also be nasty. He comments,

> Indeed, such is the nature of men in the folly of ignorance, that he presumes to teach the knowledge of things, before he knows its science. These foolish listeners are introduced to and finally led into the bliss of ignorance and into any opinions of most subtle causes of things in useless weariness. Natural philosophers *(phisici),* exalted in name only, know that 'Medicine is divided into two parts,' or that 'Life is short.'[33]

Alfred does not credit them with knowing the rest of the citation, i.e., "Art is long, opportunity fleeting, experiment treacherous, and judgment difficult."[34] Sarcastically he adds, "Having omitted the first and most eminent parts of the *Physics,* they pride themselves in having read it" (*Dmc* 51:19-52:1).

Let us now turn to some observations by Alfred on the heart. To Alfred, the heart *was* the seat of both the "spirit of life," and of the soul (*Dmc* 12:6, 14:8; 33:18): Cor est domicilium vitae. . . . Cor igitur animae domicilium est. And in his discussion of the "spirit of life," Alfred concludes, "Thus, if in fact, the generation of spirit is without time, it is, likewise, dispersed everywhere; at the same time, it is produced everywhere, and so not able to disperse *(fluere);* nor does it occupy space" (*Dmc* 51:1-4). Alfred adds, "This opinion is affirmed by the authority of Aristotle, Hippocrates, Galen, and Ysaac [Israeli], and all the most expert natural philosophers *(phisici),* but the ignorant crowd, always in error

---

traductions latines médiévales des *Météorologiques* et du *De generatione et corruptione* d'Aristote," *Revue Philosophique de Louvain* 45 (Louvain, 1947), 206–235; Minio-Paluello, "Iacobus Veneticus Grecus: Canonist and Translator of Aristotle," *Traditio* 8:265–304). Alfred's citations from these earlier Greco-Latin translations also add circumstantial evidence to my suspicion that his academic career is presently set too late.

[32] Of the authors in this category Alfred cites Boethius, *Consolation,* III metr. 9 v. 6–7 (75,16); Chalcidius, *Timaeus,* 29a (75,15); Loxus, *Phisiognomia* (87,3); Lucan, *De bello civili* II, 9–10 (77, 2–5); Seneca, *De beneficiis* I, 13,3 (4,12).

[33] This is the beginning of Honain ibn Ishak's (Johannitius) *Isagoge* of Galen's *Ars parva,* which was translated into Latin during the twelfth century and which was already known to the School of Chartres in the same century. Baeumker, *De motu cordis,* p. 51 n. 5. All subsequent references to Baeumker's edition of *De motu cordis* are given in parentheses which include the abbreviation *Dmc*.

[34] Hippocrates, *Aphorisms,* I, I, trans. W. H. S. Jones, *Hippocrates* (Cambridge, 1967), p. 99: "Life is short, the Art long, opportunity fleeting, experiment treacherous, judgment difficult."

and living apart from the truth, contradicts it" (*Dmc* 51:11-14).

In his discussion, "How the spirit of life and the principle of conception are contained in semen," Alfred says that Hippocrates in book V of the *Aphorisms* enumerates, among other things, the impediments of conception in both sexes, since "On account of the thinness of the body, the spirit is produced outside" (*Dmc* 56:1).[35]

Alfred then continues,

> Since the spermata of animals are liquid, foaming, and distended with spirit, they must be governed *(regi oportuit)* by uniform temperateness, continuous, and self-similar, and contained in a place sufficiently spacious for them to be able to expand. For all temperate things are corrupted by an intemperate overabundance, as is taught in the same *Aphorisms*. (*Dmc* 57:2-7)[36]

In his discussion of spirit *(spiritus)* Alfred distinguishes between natural spirit *(spiritus naturalis)*, and spirit of life *(spiritus vitalis vel vitae)*. To support his position he says,

> The eminent natural philosophers *(phisici)* and philosophers *(philosophi)*, Aristotle, Plato, and Ysaac [Israeli], also mention only two. Costa Lucae *filius* (i.e., Costa ben Luca), in his book, *De differentia animae et spiritus*, also demonstrates them to be only two, namely the vital and the animal spirit, and he teaches that the animal spirit owes its origin to the vital spirit. (*Dmc* 40:17-22)

At a later point, Alfred returns to this theme when he states, "Thus, the intrinsic cause of vegetation is by necessity inherent, which Alexander of Aphrodisias demonstrates in the book, *De intellectu et intellecto*."[37]

Concerning the anatomy of the heart, Alfred observes,

> Natural philosophers *(phisici)* disagree in their investigations regarding the number of its chambers. First and foremost of the anatomists, Empedocles (Abrugalis), his disciple Galen, and the entire school of physicians *(medici)* distinguish two chambers in the heart. But Aristotle, himself leading in the examinations of the other secrets of nature, has found three chambers, namely: the right one which is the place of blood *(sanguis)*, the left one which holds the air *(spiritus)*, and a middle one, which is responsible both for itself, and the amount it distributes on the other side. (*Dmc* 18:9)

---

35 Hippocrates, *Aphorisms*, V. LXIII, vol. IV, pp. 175–76. Similarly with males. Either because of the rarity of the body the breath is borne outwards so as not to force along the seed; or because of the density of the body the liquid does not pass out; or through the coldness it is not heated so as to collect at this place; or through the heat this same thing happens.

36 Ibid.

37 Baeumker, *De motu cordis*, p. 59 n. 6, explains, "This is actually from the so-called second book of the *De anima* of Alexander of Aphrodisias."

What Alfred calls Aristotle's "right and left chambers" are possibly "our" right atrium and left ventricle, while his "middle chamber" may refer to the right ventricle. Some authors state that Aristotle combined the two atria into one chamber, positing that he failed to notice the septum separating that "chamber" into "our" two atria. [38]

Unfortunately, Alfred's discussion regarding the function of the three chambers is academic, since the human heart has four chambers. He tells us that the right chamber *(dexter thalamus)* receives blood *(sanguis),* and the left chamber *(sinister thalamus)* receives air *(spiritus),* which are passed on to the middle chamber *(thalamus)* lying between the right and the left. He adds that Aristotle calls it the middle chamber *(thalamus medius),* especially since it has a large and profound concavity *(Dmc* 19:3-9; *De somno et vigilia* 458a16-19).

There seems to be no "accepted" interpretation of Aristotle's anatomy of the human heart. Permit me, therefore, to offer my own: one that conforms to both anatomy as well as function to what Alfred seems to say. Tri-chambered hearts are indeed found in amphibians, but in the case of the frog or the turtle, there are two atria and only one ventricle. I would, therefore, suggest the strong possibility that Aristotle dissected the heart of another animal, perhaps a frog or a turtle, and wrongly transferred his findings to humans. That, of course, would mean that Aristotle failed to notice the septum dividing the ventricle into two chambers in humans. But those who fault him for failing to see the septum defining the two atria are not any kinder to him.

Alfred returns to this topic at a later point. He comments,

> Some animals do not respire, in which, nonetheless, the heart is regular, and which have blood and spirit, like fish; but they suffocate when they are exposed to air, because they have no trachea. By respiring, certain [animals] also suspend taking in of air, though they are not without the spirit of life for a moment. *(Dmc* 41: 4-11)

To support his statement, he cites Galen: "Having in the thorax the proportional spirit to pulse suitably according to their size,"[39] not that Galen intends to equate air and spirit, but that it suffices for the mitigation of heat *(Dmc* 41:14).

In his chapter on the formation of the heart and the nutritive parts in the

---

[38] On the line "In animals of great size the heart has three cavities" (666b20), William Ogle, translator of the *De partibus animalium,* observes, "Commentators differ widely as to these three cavities, nor do the several passages relating to them admit of any thoroughly consistent and satisfactory interpretation. I am, however strongly of the opinion that the three are the two ventricles and the left auricle." *The Works of Aristotle,* ed. J. A. Smith and W. D. Ross, vol. V (Oxford, 1949). Baeumker, *De motu cordis,* p. 18 n. 2, echoes that view: "Der Irrtum des Aristoteles beruht wohl auf einem Übersehen der Vorhofsscheidewand."

[39] Baeumker, *De motu cordis* 41:16–18; cf. p. 24:10, and n. 2. The quote is from the *Tegni,* in the translation of Constantine the African; Kühn, ed., *Opera omnia* I (Hildesheim, 1964), cap. 11, pp. 334–35: "Multoque magis celeritas ac frequentia major fit, si thorax ad cordis proportionem auctus non fit. . . . De corporis autem universi temperamento praeterea et de thoracis latitudine ad eorum, quae ante declarata sunt, proportionem differere oportet. . . . Et risperatio, si quidem thorax cum corde proportionem habeat, eandem, quae pulsibus inest, formam servabit. . . ."

embryo, Alfred says that "Hippocrates determines the sex, as well as the health of the fetus, by the appearance of the breasts [of a pregnant woman]" (*Dmc* 71:3-5).[40]

After examining Alfred's known writings—commentaries on the *Metheora* and *De plantis*, as well as his treatise on the movement of the heart, the *De motu cordis*—one is struck by the wealth of his medical knowledge. This led Baeumker to conclude that Alfred stands outside theological thought and the determination of theological purposes. He adds,

> In some cases philosophical studies lead directly to connections outside theology; especially the study of natural sciences, which was included within the discipline of philosophy, influenced the study of medicine.[41]

Such studies served theology-centered scholastics like Thomas Aquinas (d. 1274) as a means to an end.[42] An exception was Albertus Magnus (d. 1280) who quite independently excelled as a student of natural science, as metaphysicist, and as speculative theologian. Alfred stands with Albert; his thought, likewise, is not centered in theology.[43] Only remotely related to the School of Chartres, which found its philosophical inspiration in Plato's *Timaeus*, he pursued philosophical goals based on Greco-Arabic natural philosophy and medicine. Alfred belongs to that new era which introduces high scholasticism. He combines the neo-Platonic *Weltanschauung* with the special concepts and theories of the natural philosophy of Aristotle. With the Arabs as his guides, Alfred belongs to the first generation of scholars for whom the *Liber de causis* and Avicenna, not, however, Averroes, are the determining sources.[44]

UNIVERSITY OF SAN DIEGO

---

[40] Jones, *Hippocrates, Aphorisms* V, 52, 53: "When milk flows copiously from the breasts of a women with child, it shows that the unborn child is sickly; but if the breasts are hard, it shows that the child is more healthy."

[41] Baeumker, *Stellung des Alfred,* p. 9.

[42] Ibid., p. 10.

[43] Ibid., pp. 10, 12.

[44] Ibid., pp. 63–64.

Nicolas of Cusa and the Sixth Patriarch: Reflections on Religious Discourse

by Kees W. Bolle

In the comparative study of the world's great religions, Hinduism and Buddhism stand out in presenting stories or story-like accounts parallel to philosophical expositions. Such accounts are often cast in the form of discussions between a spiritual teacher and a student. This form is of an aesthetic nature for which certainly Christianity has few examples, if any.

Or—am I exaggerating? Of course, we do have dialogues of great value, written in roughly the same time that we generally call the Middle Ages. And it will be clear from the outset that the point of this paper is not to arrive at a conclusion which one of the two, Asia or Europe, in the art of discussing issues reigns supreme. Like some of the Asian texts I have in mind, some European texts also concern themselves with the plurality of religions, religious traditions, religious perspectives, and, above all, the truth. How can we learn from both wide provinces of the human world and their concern with the question: "In what manner (or by what method) can we broach such complex issues?"

I referred to a quest for "the truth." "The truth" is a topic we are no longer in the habit of naming; we have all become "minimalists," not only as a result of academic modesty, fostered by our own modern saints, Wittgenstein, Carnap, and other philosophers who have labored in cleaning up our language, and making us aware of the significance of images underlying our views—but also by dreadful experiences in which our century has been so prolific; minimalism was forced upon us, for experiences made us painfully aware of the feebleness of our superb mental constructs.

If "the truth" is no longer a term we use freely, we ourselves have nevertheless been formed by ideas that, even if they seem to be more modest, are unmistakable pointers in some direction to which significance is attributed. I may mention the philosophy of Husserl, which, whatever else it is, is an endeavor to show the sense, the coherency of an intellectual world that by its nature says and cannot do anything else but say contradictory things; this is our intellectual world which according to Husserl in some way remains one. I may also mention Whitehead and Bergson with their central concern for processes. Much more could no doubt be mentioned by philosophers. I am a historian of religions, and for our discussion today it suffices to observe that even we have a heritage, immediately preceding our own days, that refuses a peaceful acceptance of a chaotic multiplicity as the final word; our philosophers, even in the twentieth century, say "No!" to anything that might lead to lassitude or relativism.

This having been said, we have reason to turn to some great texts of an earlier age, both East and West. And I admit that I have chosen certain texts because they seem to invite us with a special insistency. I focus in particular on passages from Nicolas of Cusa, a fifteenth-century prince of the Church, and from one Buddhist Sutra, the *Platform Sutra*. Both present discussions concerning different religious positions. Both are concerned with what is true, and despite that concern, what they actually present is, on closer inspection, not at all a simple, conceptual, dogmatic stance. In no way shall we be able to even hint in the end at the superiority of one over the other. In spite of the difference in religious structures, I do believe that we shall be able to see, perhaps with some surprise, how world-wide the concerns are with closely related issues; in some way, on some level, by some method, there is a prevailing sense, if not a unity, in the given variety of views. Questions that had come up in inter-religious discussions in the West, between Jews and Christians and Muslims, and later, for instance, between "official" Christians and "Bohemians," i.e., Hussites, do have their analogs in the East. What I expect from an examination of two very different types of texts side by side is not only more clarity in our understanding of each, but one more result: a stimulus for our locked-up specializations to bring to the attention of the entire university the force and relevance of our documents.

Discussions between and expositions of different traditions and views became inevitable in Buddhism with the rise of Mahayana, from the first few centuries of our era onward. Not by chance, as everyone knows from textbook information, the adherents of the Mahayana, "the great vehicle," coined the label "Hinayana," the "small" or rather "inferior vehicle" for the Buddhists of the old school who called themselves the "Theravadins," those who held on to the teachings of the elders. A study of such ancient discussions, and of the manner in which they were conducted, as we shall see, is highly instructive for our own manners and mannerisms in serious dialogue.

PRELIMINARIES: THE MIND AND THE SPIRIT

Each religion has something to say on what relates mind to "spirit" or man to God, and it would be wrong to suggest that the endeavor to arrive at a balanced portrayal that we shall find in Buddhism is as such unique to Buddhism. Endeavors to arrive at a balanced exposition occur in various manners and times. Ibn Kammuna was a thirteenth-century Jewish scholar in Baghdad who wrote a text in Arabic that has been praised for its fairness.[1] From early times on in the history of Christianity, splendid and impressive intellectual suggestions were made touching on the basics of all and any relation between human beings and the divine. According to St. Augustine, the image of God is certainly not directly accessible to man's sensuality, but it is present in man's ability to conceive of symmetry, which is something belonging to a properly balanced reason, not the world of the givenness of nature and senses; thus, if the senses, common to human nature as such, come to enjoy beauty in a true and correct manner, that joy derives from the inner balance transcending nature.

However, in general terms, one might say that in the history of Christianity as a whole the separation between God and man comes to the fore much more

---

[1] Moshe Perlmann, trans., *Ibn Kammuna's Examination of the Three Faiths,* praises the rationality, tolerance, and generosity of the text in terms that make Ibn Kammuna seem like a precursor of the eighteenth-century Enlightenment. See his Introduction, pp. 8–9.

often than the "traffic" between divine and human thought. By comparison, it would seem as if Buddhism has developed a very special literary architectonic.

Buddhist texts have a special paradigmatic role in discussing a paramount academic issue: the limits, task and dialectic in which the mind must be involved. The dialectic in which in Buddhism the mind must be involved is indeed crucial to the discussion of variety and conflict in religious lore.

The problem of a relation between mind and what is more than mind arises at once from the most elementary description of Buddhism. The monk trains the direction of his mind away from worldly attachments, he purifies it, turns it to non-attachment, disciplining it toward something beyond ordinary mental habits. When, in 1989, the Dalai Lama learned he was to receive the Nobel Peace Prize, he expressed his surprise and said: "I am only a monk." This was of course not a feigned reaction. It was an example of what the discipline of meditating brings about, away from the normal vagaries of thought and desire. The advanced monk is a spiritual man. As academics, we know about those things, but we do not, *qua* academics, purify ourselves in that manner. The practicing "spiritual" person knows a "way." We labor with the mind.

Working with the mind—that is what universities are for. And primarily from this place, from our university perspective, we are puzzled and intrigued by the spiritual life.

One inevitable problem for us involves precisely: our individual minds. It is a problem of long standing. We spend our time, virtually all our time, working with the mind, and while doing so we wonder collectively about the nature of "the spiritual life." The mind, to which we are so used, so habituated, so addicted, is not a microscope in which one can turn the light on or off at will. And if one could turn off its light, after the manner of a microscope, one would not thereby automatically transcend the mind and move into the realm of the spirit. What is their relationship, then?

LINKAGE IN HISTORY

In this context, there are very good reasons for speaking of religion and universities, "the spirit" and the mind, as linked. This linkage is well-known, though it does not receive the attention it deserves.

In virtually all of Western history we see that universities began with Theology: Paris, Prague, Göttingen, Leiden, etc. (Padua is exceptional, having started with Law.) And even in the United States, the older universities, before the land began to teem with state institutions, set out with Divinity schools: Harvard, Yale, Princeton, Chicago, and Columbia with its Union Theological Seminary are historically not far removed from the same tradition.

In Asia, history shows comparable examples. Pataliputra, Nalanda, Lhasa and many other cities gained fame as Buddhist seats of learning. That is where one went for higher education. Kenneth J. Saunders wrote a book on periods in the history of Buddhism, and he did so principally by discussing successive intellectual centers of florescence in India, Ceylon, Burma, Thailand, China, Korea, Japan, Nepal, and Tibet.[2]

Historical facts of this sort are important. They remind us of the religious origins of our institutionalized intellectual life. Without the religious group around Pythagoras, an important stimulus for developing number systems would have been missing. And we probably owe a great deal to Buddhism in developing for its undeniably religious purposes the concept of zero.

Nevertheless, I wish to look at something more important than such sheer historical relationships. The facts are that they're not by accident, but because of a fundamental reality of which they are the signs.

"The mind and the spirit" is the general name I give to a fundamental reality that has confronted men and women who have been working with their minds from ancient days on. The New Testament speaks of *metanoia*. It is loosely translated as "conversion." The term itself conveys the meaning of a redirection of the mind. And the tone and wording of the biblical texts make very clear that the issue of such a change is not merely a discovery that the mind makes by itself. Any real change comes from the one "who has established his throne in heaven" (Psalm 103:19). The book of Isaiah has God himself saying: ". . . my thoughts are not your thoughts, and your ways are not my ways. This is the very word of the Lord. For as the heavens are higher than the earth, so are my ways higher than your ways and my thoughts than your thoughts . . ." (Is. 55:8–9). And in prayer, one says to that divine king: ". . . you understand my thought . . ." (Psalm 139:2). Our thought by itself does not bring about a relation to that supreme sovereign. "Which of you by taking thought can add one cubit to his height?" (Matt. 6:27; Luke 12:25).

Among the most famous episodes in the earliest history of Buddhism is that of the conversion of Sariputta and Moggallana. Their story alerts us to the necessary relation between mind and spirit most dramatically, aesthetically, and acutely.

The two were wandering ascetics, part of a large group assembled under a teacher. They had set their minds on "finding the deathless." And these two had made a promise to each other: that whoever would find the deathless first would tell the other. It is Sariputta's good fortune, one morning, on his rounds for alms, to meet one of the Buddha's disciples, Assaji. Sariputta is struck by him at once, as is everyone who first sets eyes on him. For Assaji's begging is more than ordinary begging. He entered the city (Rajagaha), "winning the minds of men with his advancing and his retiring, with his looking and his gazing, with his drawing in his arms and his stretching out his arms, and having his eyes cast down, and perfect in his deportment."[3] The sight of Assaji makes Sariputta wonder: Is this just a monk? Or already a saint? Shouldn't I go and ask him: Who is your teacher? Who is the one for whose teachings you decided to withdraw from the world?

---

[2] Kenneth J. Saunders, *Epochs in Buddhist History,* The Haskell Lectures, 1921 (Chicago, 1924).

[3] The story is related in Henry Clarke Warren, *Buddhism in Translations* (New York, 1974), pp. 87–91.

Sariputta knows it is not proper to disturb a monk within the city, going the rounds for alms. He waits for Assaji to be done, and then approaches him and raises his question:

> Placid, brother, are all your organs of sense; clear and bright is the color of your skin. To follow whom, brother, did you retire from the world? Who is your teacher? and whose doctrine do you approve?

Assaji identifies his teacher, the Buddha, Sakyamuni. Then, with truthfulness and humility, he broaches the teachings. He says:

> . . . I am a novice and a newcomer, and the time is but short since I retired from the world under this Doctrine and Discipline [of the Buddha]. I am not able to expound to you on the Doctrine at any great length, but I can tell you the substance of it in brief.

Of course Sariputta urges him to disclose this doctrine, no matter how briefly. And then he sums up his understanding in a couple of verses, as follows:

> The Buddha has the causes told
> Of all things springing from a cause;
> And also how things cease to be—
> 'Tis this the Mighty Monk proclaims.

On hearing this exposition of the Doctrine, there arose in the mind of Sariputta, the wandering ascetic, a clear and distinct perception of the Doctrine that whatever is subject to origination is also subject to cessation. "If this is the Doctrine," said he, "then indeed have you reached the sorrowless state lost sight of and neglected by many myriads of world-cycles."

The simplicity of grasping what is ungraspable for the ordinary mind is the point of the story. And in order not to allow the point to be lost, the story goes on to tell us how Sariputta, true to his promise, at once seeks out his fellow wanderer Moggallana; he tells Moggallana of his encounter, concludes by repeating the verse the disciple of the Buddha recited to him, and at once, Moggallana too is overcome with joy. Both have attained the deathless.

This story is vivid, yet it would not suffice to admire it for its aesthetic qualities. The story leads us to the serious issue at hand.

Those religious stories, as much a part of history as the economic, political, military events that our mind is in the habit of sizing up, come closer to the great problem that intrigues, perplexes, and vexes us until this very day. Many of the seemingly so elevated inquiries that we engage in are no more than a camouflage for this central problem. Those inquiries entail our quest for what unites the many religions and peoples of the world, and entail also the everlasting noble concern as to the value of a university education. The central problem in all of this is the most difficult to deal with: How can we do anything of importance with the mind, if the mind itself has no worthwhile direction? This is the question at the root of all the others: What is it that is able to unite peoples? What sense does education have? Why such lack of balance, such chaos in the curricula of colleges?

THE SEARCH FOR WISDOM

"Wisdom" is a term commonly used in translations of Buddhist texts: *prajña*. We do not often use the term "wisdom" in ordinary academic conversation. And yet, the sensible statements and the sensible story we have just referred to all say something that can hardly be denied. The term *sapientia* occurs in our texts, and "wisdom" is one of the terms that cannot fail to come up in our minds when we try to describe Cusanus's *docta ignorantia*. And in the same area, the word *prajña* is found.

Knowledge rests on something, but not after the manner of one block resting on another. Rather, the acquisition of knowledge rests on, receives its orientation from an inquiry distinct from itself. Its own movement derives from that, and so does its own doubt, its own daring to engage in its own dialectic.

The West developed its own mechanisms to push away the problem of reason and spirit. In each case the "and spirit" part seemed to get eliminated. I am not at all saying that such a thing has happened only in the West. But realizing that we have nothing but our minds to work with is not the same as being only at home in our minds. The discoveries that set our minds thinking originate elsewhere; not infrequently in the wilds, the deserts, and in short, in homelessness.

Thinking of the development of our universities and their mental efforts in the nineteenth century, the image that comes to my mind is that of an old-fashioned governor, governing a colonized region of the world. Like most governors, he was in charge, using all his mental efforts to remain in charge, and not infrequently he was accompanied on his compound by a missionary; they were both at home in their mind. This was the situation in India, and I am often afraid that it is still the situation of the modern powerful university, its organization and its use of the mind. By contrast, it is useful to consider that the future Buddha was first called to go forth not only by the visions of an old man, a sick man, and a dead man, but also by a monk, a homeless wanderer by definition. Without any need for an elaboration on the sociology of knowledge, let us realize that our modern university's scientific occupations have grown up in a cozy, bourgeois environment. That is our mind's current domicile. The roots of the great religious traditions are firmly set in an intellectual soil of a very different compost. Buddhism points the way toward Enlightenment from the outset under the image of homelessness.

The relationship of mind and spirit is always revealing, and certainly surprising each time it manifests itself. Here the religious texts speak up, loud and clear.

A FRAGMENT FROM THE *PLATFORM SUTRA*

I would now like to look at a passage from the *Platform Sutra*. I have no intention to suggest that what I see expressed here is the only thing expressed;

it is not as if the text were written with the purpose of solving the great epistemological crisis of our age and our university. However, its teachings encompass our problem eloquently.

The central speaker in the text is known as the Sixth Patriarch: Hui-neng (eighth century A.D.), the great teacher who stands at the cradle of Ch'an or Zen Buddhism. The passage I am interested in here introduces the monk Fa-ta. We are told that he has been reciting the *Lotus Sutra* continuously for seven years. However, "his mind was still deluded and he did not know where the true Dharma lay."[4] He goes to the mount where Hui-neng, the Master, resides, and begs him to resolve his doubts. The Master answers:

> Fa-ta, you are very proficient in the Dharma, but your mind is not proficient. You may have no doubts in so far as the sutras are concerned (but your mind itself doubts). You are searching for the true Dharma with falsehood in your mind. If your own mind were correct and fixed, you would be a man who has taken the sutra to himself. I have never in my life known written words, but if you bring a copy of the *Lotus Sutra* and read it to me, upon hearing it, I will understand it at once.

Fa-ta brings the sutra and reads it to the Master in its entirety. And of course, the Master does understand the Buddha's meaning, and he proceeds to explain it to Fa-ta:

> Fa-ta, the *Lotus Sutra* does not say anything more than is needed. Throughout all its seven Chüan [scrolls] it gives parables and tales about causation. The Tathagata's preaching of the Three Vehicles was only because of the dullness of people in the world. The words of the sutra clearly state that there is only one vehicle of Buddhism and that there is no other vehicle.

The issue is quite familiar; it is the question of the given multiplicity of the world we are in and the unity, the simplicity we seek in understanding. It is also the question of our scholarship, our labor with the mind over all the phenomena we single out and pile up for our specializations, and the quest for the sense of them.

The Master goes on with his explanation. The core is a quotation that seems puzzling when we first hear it: "Let me explain to you. The Sutra says: The various Buddhas and the World-honored One appeared in this world because of the one great causal event." However, the text itself affirms the importance of the statement by adding: "The above sixteen characters are the true Dharma." Continuing his explanation, the Master says something that does not fit neatly into Fa-ta's knowledge of the *Lotus Sutra,* or for that matter, into our scholarly mind-schemes either. Hui-neng says:

---

[4] I am following the text from the translation by Philip B. Yampolsky, *The Platform Sutra of the Sixth Patriarch: The Text of the Tun-Huang Manuscript* (New York, 1967), pp. 165–8.

> The mind has nothing to do with thinking, because its fundamental source is empty. To discard false views, this is the one great causal event. If within and without you are not deluded then you are apart from duality. If on the outside you are deluded you cling to form; if on the inside you are deluded you cling to emptiness. *If within form you are apart from form and within emptiness you are separated from emptiness then within and without you are not deluded.*[5]

"To discard false views, this is the one great causal event." We must realize of course that discarding false views does not refer to our mind's work, our science, attaining some final perfection. Attainment of our real goal does not depend on spinning out our thoughts further and further on their wonted course. On the contrary—it depends not on a Euclidean proof, but on the sort of thing we shun in science, something resembling a paradox—and yet, a paradox not of an irrational sort à la Kirkegaard, but of an experienced and sensible reality. In the New Testament, there is the statement about being in, but not of the world. However, the *Platform Sutra* is far more explicit in its applicability to the mental activity we are engaged in. "Emptiness" and "form" are the opposites. Our thoughts depend on forms in which they are expressed and on which we rely. We are made aware of something else, the peculiar "opposite" that seems to escape all mental definition on which our "forms" depend. Yet that very opposite is not really or not merely an opposite, precisely because of our mind's dependence on it for its proper task: to discard false views and attain purity.

To rephrase the matter in a way that is useful for our academic consumption: We should not imagine that we can get a scientific hold on the "ultimate reality." [We should not reduce it to a concept of the mind.] We should not hold on even to our most precious scientific ideas or findings as if they were the key to salvation. *If within form you are apart from form and within emptiness you are separated from emptiness, then within and without you are not deluded.*

If much against my wishes I have seen fit to transform a perfectly clear teaching into a highfalutin' intellectualism, let me add another quote from Hui-neng: "Fa-ta, it is my constant wish that all the people in the world will always themselves open the wisdom of the Buddha in their own mind-grounds." If I may continue my simile: our mental domicile becomes useful only by directing itself to what comes from homelessness.

And finally, let us remember one detail of the story of Hui-neng teaching a monk whose mind was not proficient: it was this unproficient monk who did all the academically required mind-work and studied the *Lotus Sutra* for seven years, reciting it continuously. The Sixth Patriarch who opened it up for him was the one who did not know the text. He had never in his life known written words.

---

[5] Italics added.

NICHOLAS OF CUSA'S *DE PACE FIDEI*

On Nicolas of Cusa I can be brief in the company of medievalists. He lived seven centuries after Hui-neng. Contemporaneousness is not of great significance for our present purpose. We might even argue that both were key figures in a renaissance: the one that saw the beginnings of revolutionary, wide understanding of Christian teachings as well as of modern science, and the one that saw in the beginnings of Zen Buddhism a comparable revolutionary spaciousness.

Cusanus was directly concerned with the problem of multiple religious claims. The treatise known as *De pace fidei* begins with the description of a confused man, and it is not hard to guess that it is autobiographical. I suppose that the title should be translated into our world more correctly as *The Peace of Religions* than *The Peace of Faith*. The translators Deitlind and Wilheim Dupré follow somewhat of a middle course: *Der Friede im Glauben*.[6] Thereby, quite correctly, they point to the central purpose: an "ultimate" peace, philosophically transparent and politically normative at the same time.

The protagonist is confused—worse than that, he is *zelo Dei accensus,* 'ignited with zeal before God,' as a result of the horrors brought about by the reports of the Turks in Constantinople; he fervently prays God for a vision. Not only Islam's advances, but the dissensions of all religious traditions are on his mind. At last, the vision is granted to him, revealing the hoped-for final peace. The God of Heaven and Earth is most certainly aware of all that is happening. Under the chairmanship of no one less than the *Verbum Dei,* an assembly is set up consisting of spiritual representatives of all religions.

What the author sees is a vision, in a dream. Recently, a scholar has pointed out the striking function of dreams in some medieval dialogues concerning "the truth" in religions.[7] She refers to the significant role of dreams in the twelfth-century dialogue *The Kuzari* by a Spanish Jew, Judah Halevi, and in another one by Peter Abelard, in the same century. Abelard has a dream, which he records in his *Dialogue of a Philosopher with a Jew, and a Christian*. A personal communication by the same scholar who looked at these texts doubts the value of theoretical literary speculation concerning dreams. Rather, dreams of such issues as interreligious discussion, she argues, should be seen as an attractive alternative to a systematic exposition of a scale of values governing the relative merit of Judaism, Christianity, Islam, and Paganism. For our discussion, this suggestion seems indeed worth mentioning. What a later age occasionally wanted to establish fully systematically, factually, could at times be apprehended in the Middle Ages as needing the open-ended quality characteristic of dreams.

---

[6] Leo Gabriel, ed., Dietlind Dupré and Wilhelm Dupré, trans., *Nikolaus von Kues, Philosophisch-theologische Schriften,* 3 Vols. (Vienna, 1967).

[7] See Sara Denning-Bolle, "Christian Dialogue as Apologetic: The Case of Justin Martyr seen in Historical Context," in *Bulletin of the John Ryland University Library of Manchester* 69 (1987), 507.

The ensuing debate in the vision of *De pace fidei* shows us that the Austrian Nicolas of Cusa was remarkably well aware of claims and assumptions even in distant traditions. For example, the *Indus* speaks of the great significance of statues and images in true worship. Likewise, the Greek, Persian, Chaldean, less surprisingly of course the Arab, and others take the floor, displaying equally precise traits.

Remains the fact that the *Verbum Dei* presides and in fact is the one who presents all the answers. Still—we are in a dream. The key, which of course all medievalists are thoroughly familiar with in Nicolas of Cusa, is the perfection of each thing in itself, if only it is truly itself. This key rings true to every Hindu, and to every Buddhist as well.

I do not want to leave the impression that Nicolas of Cusa gave us all the answers. Perhaps the Christian framework has in its very structure a special problem of having to establish a hierarchy of truths. In a small treatise by Nicolas of Cusa on the Koran, in spite of all harmonizing efforts, we do read statements that leave no doubt in this regard. For instance, real Scripture can be only Christian Scripture; thus, in Cusanus' words, "The Koran is not worthy of faith in places where it contradicts the Sacred Scriptures"; and quite straightforwardly, "The Gospel is preferable to the Koran." Those statements, however, do not prevent Cusanus from granting some measure of divine truthfulness to the Koran. And in the same manner he grants truth to all religious traditions presented in *De pace fidei*.

The method—or dream—of Cusanus takes an honorable place next to the *Platform Sutra's* presentation. I admit that the Buddhist text in my taste is aesthetically more appealing. Obviously, the discussion between the Sixth Patriarch and Fa-Ta displays a sense of humor that is difficult to find parallels to in the West. However, it is particularly noteworthy that the Sutra as a whole makes references to the three distinct Buddhist traditions—and, of course, only one is truly the highest. Up to a point, such a differentiation does seem analogous to the hierarchy that Cusanus also upholds. However, the Buddhist text in one respect goes an important step further; not so much by arguing, but by depicting the spiritual struggle toward Enlightenment, the different forms of Buddhism become very much like stages in the spiritual journey. The question of truth or untruth does not seem to come up with equal urgency.

However, with this final statement I have already come too close to what I said I was not going to do: there is no reason for placing Buddhism and Christianity in some absolute hierarchic graph, one with respect to the other. Rather, the most imposing thing is that in both traditions we find patient, contemplating endeavors to shy away from any such absolutism in evaluation. Instead, as Karl Jaspers argued in a variety of ways in his book on Nicolas of Cusa, there is every reason to pay full attention to the necessity of allowing for the transcendent to remain transcendent. This is the lesson, both East and West, that we have to rediscover anew, whatever material we have chosen for our "specialty."

UNIVERSITY OF CALIFORNIA, LOS ANGELES

Medieval Concepts and Their Resonance: An Introduction

by James Porter

The papers that follow represent views of Eastern and Western modal and generic concepts, their points of intersection and divergence. Doris Stockmann's paper provides a broad framework for the presentations since it interprets, from an ethnomusicological as well as an historical standpoint, Johannes de Grocheio's concept of *musica vulgaris* that was based, apparently, on indigenous musical traditions in France during the thirteenth century. This was a period when the urban classes began to develop new forms of secular musical life, not only in France but in contiguous areas. The term has been glossed as *musica simplex vel civilis,* which may mean, as Heinrich Besseler thought, one-part social music *(einstimmig-umgangsmässige Musik).* Others such as Johannes Wolf and Ernst Rohloff, who edited Grocheio's texts, took *civilis* to mean *bürgerlich, vulgaris* to signify *volkstümlich* but *simplex* to refer not to *einstimmig* (one-part), but to *einfach* (simple), a meaning that Dr. Stockmann prefers since *einstimmig* could be misinterpreted as pure unison. At any rate, *musica vulgaris* included the refrain forms of the *rondeau, virelais,* and *ballade; trouvère* genres; non-Latin spiritual songs of epic or lyric character; and new instrumental genres that included both dances and pieces for listening.

The text by Grocheio offers three pointers in explicating *musica vulgaris:* the close relationship between vocal and instrumental genres in his classification system; the issue of orality and the fact of oral genres being first included in written works about this time; and the problem of tonality, which was not bound by ecclesiastical rules. Dr. Stockmann emphasizes that *musica vulgaris* is a complex term used to cover various kinds of music: orally-transmitted vocal genres of town and country; professional genres that were becoming more folklike and popular with the growth of towns; didactic or school songs; and artistic genres intended for people of wealth and privilege. One genre is not mentioned by Grocheio: the paraliturgical spiritual song with vernacular words, usually associated with pilgrims or flagellants (Italian *laude,* German *Geisslerleider),* probably because of papal edict against popular motets. This music, then, *musica vulgaris,* was loosely unified in performance (not necessarily in unison), indigenous, and vernacular. As such it includes a wide range of music—urban, rural, amateur, professional, secular, sacred—that appealed to different classes.

Most of these genres crossed national boundaries, into the Iberian peninsula, into Germany, Italy, Britain and Ireland. Later and further afield, the Caribbean shows traces of French influence in the dance songs *juba, bele (bel air)* and *calenda,* though in the *tumba francesca* and *quadrilles* of the nineteenth century, direct proof of French ancestry is problematic. Four Philippine musical terms in particular have their basis in the Spanish colonial period: *banda* (wind band), *rondalla* (plucked string ensemble), *kundiman* (national art song derived from an earlier folk genre, an improvised dance song), and *sarswela* (popular opera derived from the Hispanic *zarzuela*). The *rondalla* (Grocheio's *rotundellus* or *rondellus*), the string ensemble, seems in particular to echo the concept of *musica vulgaris* in its function as a cultural emblem, while the *banda* is quite possibly a reminder of the open-air music for *tympanum et tuba* (trumpet and drum) in the medieval treatise. In addition, the Portuguese in Brazil, who among other things took with them older Galician traditions, did not have categorical differences in their music such as "art," "popular," or "folk." The meetings of *trovadores,* improvising singers (usually in pairs) in the southeast and midwest of Brazil, is an adaptation of the competitions of the eleventh- and twelfth-century troubadour that developed in the municipalities of Grocheio's time.

José Maceda's paper takes up the issue of bipolarity, the tonal importance of the fifth degree, or dominant note, as an historical process that came about in the sixteenth and seventeenth centuries, in the West, with the use of harmony and the discovery of equal temperament. In early organum there is no clear relationship between octaves, fifths and fourths since the parts simply followed the principal voice, though one can find the use of a bipolar leading tone in the compositions of Guillaume de Machaut. The tonic or ending tone had to be emphasized, and this was gradually brought about through the technique of bipolarity.

In the Javanese gamelan, in contrast, we encounter a musical universe built on pentatonic structures, one found in both court and folk music. Dual pentatonic scales in Southeast Asia indicate an indigenous theory and practice different from the theory of fifth cycles in China. The Javanese gamelan *slendro* has whole-tone steps, *pelog* half-tone steps, and although there are seven tones in *pelog*, only five are used at any one time. Melodies constructed on these scales rely on traditional cadential formulas and ending tones that identify the character of the music *(pathet)*. Of the five tones used in *pelog* and *slendro,* one is used less frequently or avoided, so that there remain just four tones played in the music of all *pathet*, and these four tones are related to one another by the fifth degree or its inversion, the fourth. As Dr. Maceda observes, all five tones in *slendro* and five tones at a time in *pelog* are root structures in which each tone has equal weight or importance in relation to each other. Within this pentatonic structure and relation of fifth falls the application of two techniques, "bipolarity" and "counts of four," that provide structural organization to the music.

"Counts of four" is a basic device encountered not only in Javanese and Balinese gamelan but in other Southeast Asian musics such as the flat gong ensembles of the Philippines and Vietnam, in the Malay Peninsula, North Sumatra, Javanese village folk music, Mindanao, Borneo and Thailand. Culturally, of course, the number four is symbolized in the square, and examples of the concept of four can be found in the structure of Buddhist temples and in the Borodudur in Java, in which the body of the temple consists of five square terraces, diminishing in size, while the top is made up of narrowing circular terraces. Four, then, is a symbol in cosmological interpretation and material construction, and it is also heard in gamelan music as proportions of counting. Examples are provided to illustrate this important point.

It is worth noting that in *pelog,* the use of half steps and a wide range of pitches between intervals do not affect bipolarity and the fifth interval, since these two elements are still the basic structure of those intervals. Whereas in Western music, too, the play of opposition, contrast and complement became clearer historically when the role of the fifth was clarified in relation to its tonic, in gamelan the fifth interval is a built-in mechanism that facilitates bipolarity. The goal of these means, however, is ambiguous since the choices of ending are limited, and choosing one or the other is where equivocation arises. Cadences and a restricted number of ending *gongan* (melodic cycle) tones amount to a technique that gives a sense of order to these tones, subjected as they are to counts of four and bipolarity. The same basic elements, counts of four, bipolarity and the fifth interval, are characteristic of a widespread region of music that also includes Thailand and Cambodia.

The third paper, by Nancy van Deusen, is on the medieval sequence, and examines in particular two examples from the Central European rather than Frankish region in order to establish its generic individuality. This results, she asserts, primarily from its static style which in itself speaks to an anachronistic value-system in its later phase (after 1300). Dr. van Deusen considers several key questions relating to essential melodic style and distinctive structural moments; how can these be described and analyzed? She also focuses on the issue of what a complete, composed sequence is, or might be. These problems in turn lead to a consideration of text-music relationships, and the suggestion that personal and subjective tastes should be minimized in any analysis of structural validity.

In illustrating her argument she compares the examples *Rex regum Deus noster colende,* notated in the late thirteenth century from the manuscript Kassel, Landesbibliothek 4°5, and *Promissa mundo gaudia,* dating from the twelfth century and copied well into the sixteenth; the edition source is the *Franus Cantionale* from Hradec Králové in Southern Bohemia (c. 1505). The first sequence has a limited tonal vocabulary, with emphasis on pentatonic aspects of the entire ambitus of an extended octave *c–d'.* The most distinctive feature is the rhythmic stress that is produced by textual rather than musical accent. Yet this results in a bond between tone and syllable, a unity of style, that is not present in the later sequence. Pattern and device, both textual and musical, draw interest away from the unity of word and tone. Distinctive and overt devices move the sequence away from its liturgical purpose towards autonomous "composition."

Yet in some ways the same stylistic features are present: a process of musical extension that is additive rather than developmental; there is no well-defined musical goal, and this links it on one level to the ambiguity of the gamelan cadence formulas. The sequence's ceremonial purpose, of course, helped to define its musical and textual style. Its transitional function between the *alleluia* and *gospel* created a bridge within the Mass, but the sequence also, in a wider symbolic sense, embodies a bridge to other musical traditions that do not rely on arresting beginnings and teleological development (those of Indonesia, for example).

The correspondences among these three papers are as striking as the divergences. On the one hand they are dealing with quite different aspects of musical behavior, from the interpretation of key terminology (Stockmann) to the structural functions of counts of four, bipolarity and the fifth interval in gamelan (Maceda) and the relative stylistic stasis of the medieval church sequence over three centuries (van Deusen). Yet the papers are linked by their reaching out beyond the confines of particularistic scholarship to suggest wider links with other music cultures, and in so doing to renew a valuable tradition of cross-cultural investigation that has too often been devalued in comparison with research on a specific period or style (and thereby moving, I am tempted to say, into the conceptual territory of ethnomusicology).

Dr. Stockmann's paper suggests the need to rethink our inadequate categories of "art," "folk," and "popular" in accordance with Grocheio's far-sighted view of *music vulgaris,* a concept some might render as "vernacular music" (although there is no adequate term in English), and shows how the concept has spread in many transformative ways to the New World. Dr. Maceda's study of gamelan indicates how pentatonic structures (or tetratonic ones) can be organized in inventive sequences that nevertheless lead to tonal ambiguity in cadential concepts. This lack of directedness, or ateleological characteristic of gamelan is shared with the medieval church sequence, though one should be aware of making too close a parallel. The comparability of tonal means does not necessarily indicate homologous tonal concepts, and ethnomusicologists have rightly cautioned against speculation on the presence of pentatonic structures in different parts of the world. For one thing, the organization of the gamelan's and the sequence's melodic shapes is structurally divergent. Even though to the Western ear they both seem to hint at otherworldliness by means of a "disembodied" sound texture, and the tonal material of both gives the impression of circling rather than linear directedness, the worldview that lies behind them is difficult to compare.

The multiple cycles of gamelan music are related, in the first instance, to a comparable system of calendrical cycles. The meanings of calendrical cycles in a person's life are important and complex in an astrological sense, and some scholars, the Beckers in particular,[1] have argued that the metaphoric linkage is one of the significant ways in which artistic forms take on meaning. As pitches coincide at important structural points in gamelan music, so certain days coincide to mark important moments in one's personal life. Calendrical cycles relate, ultimately, to the realm of nature and the heaven's cycles, and gamelan music has an "iconic" relationship with the same realm. To extract richer meanings from the coincidence of calendrical cycles, one adds more

---

[1] Judith and Alton Becker, "A Musical Icon: Power and Meaning in Javanese Gamelan Music," in *The Sign in Music and Literature,* ed. Wendy Steiner (Austin, 1981), pp. 203–15.

cycles until an overlay of cycles marks an expansion process that sometimes results in *kenongan* (primary subcycle of a *gongan*, named for the *kenong,* a set of large horizontal pot gongs) and *gongan* of astonishing length in which as many as ten layers of melody coincide at *kenong.* Musical coincidences, moreover, are iconic with at least one other realm in Java besides the cosmic/calendrical realm, that is, the realm of human relationships: the plots of the shadow-puppet play reflect the same overlay of cycles.

The *gongan* structure, then, is fundamental to Javanese music, and its coherence is conceived around time, the seasons, and one's personal fate. In contrast, the medieval church sequence presents numerous problems, both of genesis and performance. Specialists such as Crocker[2] have pointed to the inconclusive nature of the evidence on performance during the period in which it flourished. Its importance as a genre is not in doubt, yet there are special problems of context and meaning still to be solved: was its stationary quality, as Dr. van Deusen observes, the main reason for its disappearance from the Mass? Is its meaning something that can be extracted from the structure and style of its circumscribed historical evolution, or is it dependent in some degree on ecclesiastical ideology and on the analysis of performance context? These questions are not merely speculative, surely, but ones that must, as in this symposium, continue to engage scholars of living music and of historically significant genres in both East and West.

UNIVERSITY OF CALIFORNIA, LOS ANGELES

---

[2] Richard L. Crocker, *The Early Medieval Sequence* (Berkeley, 1977).

The Medieval Concept and Genres of *musica vulgaris:* Influences outside of Europe?

by Doris Stockmann

The export of medieval concepts and genres of popular and folk music from Europe to other parts of the world could have taken place in different periods. The most important of them is probably the first one: the great epoch of colonization and Christian missionary activity from the end of the fifteenth century onwards by the Spanish, Portuguese, French, British and Dutch conquerors; later on also by other European countries. Although I will concentrate here on this period, because I want to discuss the medieval concept and genres of *musica vulgaris*, questioning whether or not there are traces to be found outside Europe, let me touch briefly on some later periods of European export of people, as well as ideas, customs, and music.

There is, for instance, the selling of soldiers to North America in the last decades of the eighteenth century, mainly from Germany, or the big emigration waves from several European countries, beginning shortly after 1600. Another emigration climax occurred from the middle of the nineteenth century onwards, when economic calamity and political pressure (after the unsuccessful revolution of 1848–49) forced hundreds of thousands of peasants, craftsmen and workers to leave their homelands for the New World.[1]

Concerning the musical traditions of these people, they were, at least partially, bound to the old strata of European folk music or included genres with medieval roots, for example English and Scottish popular ballads, which in the New World preserved more ancient traits than they did in Europe.[2] The immigration status and difficulty adapting to it caused people to preserve their homeland traditions in a specific, conservative way; the developments which eventually took place may have progressed in totally different directions than did simultaneous developments in the homeland. Philip Bohlman mentions the fact that in many areas of German settlement in the American Midwest, hymns and other religious genres passed from written sources to oral tradition within several generations, thereafter constituting the largest body of folk music for many German-American communities.[3]

Quite a different example—although not yet verified—could be taken from legal practice and jurisdiction, where in North America, as well as in medieval Europe, a few musical or quasi-musical utterances are or were involved. Some ten to fifteen years ago, I did some interesting research on

---

[1] Wolfgang Steinitz, *Volkslieder demokratischen Charakters aus sechs Jahrhunderten* I (Berlin, 1954), 116ff, 455, 465.

[2] Bertrand Harris Bronson, *The Traditional Tunes of the Child Ballads* (Princeton, 1959–72).

[3] *The Study of Folk Music in the Modern World* (Chicago, 1988), p. 57.; "Hymnody in the Rural German-American Community of the Upper Midwest," *The Hymn* 35:3 (1984), 158–64.

German medieval legal sources.[4] I learned that several kinds of official signaling (by voice or instruments) were present in everyday life during the Middle Ages and the beginning of modern times in order to tell people what they had to do. And there were, twice or three times a year, oral recitations of the law for illiterate people, interwoven with musically influenced passages in order to facilitate its remaining in memory of the audience. Legal affairs (trade, selling, auctions, etc.) and legal actions of any kind were framed by or interspersed with small musical details. I have asked myself whether, for example, the special vocal performance of the speakers in a Midwest auction of cattle, or in the stock exchange in former times, or in old-fashioned jurisdiction—as one may watch it in a Western movie recounting a story from the last century—might have their roots in these well-documented medieval practices in Central Europe. As I said, more proof is desirable, but to me it would be rather strange if there did not exist some connection.

One could collect and present more of such examples; I will not set forth in this way now, but will go back first to the European Middle Ages to show a certain concept and certain types of "popular" musical genres which developed as a new species at the very beginning of modern times. By their special character, these genres could have had the power, at least in principle, not only to survive, but also to fertilize musical developments outside their homelands.

Musica vulgaris is a special term in medieval music theory, as is *cantus vulgaris* in the theory of literature. Both occur first in Latin sources of French and Italian origin around 1300, and later on (up to the sixteenth century) also in theoretical writings of other Roman Catholic countries in Europe, for example, in Germany. Right from the beginning, the term revealed a strongly programmatic character, mainly in the well-known musical treatise we will discuss presently—that of Johannes de Grocheio (Grocheo)—but also in other famous sources of the time, for instance Dante's treatise *De vulgari eloquentia* (written between 1304 and 1308). Since modern musicology has not yet clearly shown what the *musica vulgaris* really is, I have tried to develop a new interpretation.[5]

---

[4] "Deutsche Rechtsdenkmäler des Mittelalters als volksmusikalische Quelle," *Studia musicologica* 15 (1973), 267–302; "Der Kampf um die Glocken im deutschen Bauernkrieg," *Beiträge zur Musikwissenschaft* 16 (1974), 163–93; "Die Erforschung vokaler und instrumentaler Praktiken im mittelalterlichen Rechtsleben," *Deutsches Jahrbuch der Musikwissenschaft für 1973–1977* (Leipzig, 1978), pp. 115–34.

[5] Concerning the analysis of Grocheio's treatise, see the extensive quotation of literature in my study "Musica vulgaris bei Johannes de Grocheo," *Beiträge zur Musikwissenschaft* 25 (Berlin, 1983), 3–56. Also see "Musica vulgaris im französischen Hochmittelalter: Johannes de Grocheio in neuer Sicht," *Historische Volksmusikforschung* (*Tagungsbreicht Limassol 1982, Study Group on Historical Sources of ICTM*), ed. Alois Mauerhofer, *Musiktechnologische Sammelbände* 7 (Graz, 1985), 163–179; "Von der Chanson de geste zur Herausbildung folklorisierter Erzähllied-Gattungen im Hochmittelalter," in *årsbok för Vis och Folkmusikforskning* (Stockholm, 1986), pp. 114–134. For an edition and translation of the treatise, see especially Ernst Rohloff, *Die Quellenhandschriften zum Musiktraktat des*

It was around the turn of the fourteenth century that progressive parts of the young medieval *Stadtbürgertum* developed new trends and forms of secular musical life. This was also true for northern Italy as well as for northern France and southern Britain. In France and the Anglo-Norman regions, for instance, the so-called *puys* came into being: municipal societies of musicians and people interested in music, including bourgeois intellectuals, as well as noblemen and clerics. The still-existing troubadour and trouvère traditions changed, at least partly, from the former courtly contexts into these new kinds of competitive musical societies. At the same time, a purely instrumental music making rapidly developed. And the old *chanson de geste*—to take another example—lost its former character of noblemen's and knights' poetry, as had been the case during the Crusades, and became a new kind of entertainment for lower- and middle-class people in the growing cities.

Johannes de Grocheo—or, as his name appears in the manuscript, Grocheio—is one of the very few witnesses who mediates some insight into these highly interesting processes of musical history. About his life and personality we know almost nothing. He lived in Paris before or around 1300, and it is suggested that he, as *regens Parisius*, had an educational appointment at the *Collegium Sorbonnicum*. This *Collegium*, the University of Paris (Sorbonne), had existed at this time for about one hundred years, and it was then, of course, a purely theological college. Grocheio paid his tribute to this very fact by including a detailed description of the *musica ecclesiastica*, but he did it in a somewhat unusual way due to his realistic and enlightened way of thinking.

Apparently, his charge at the Sorbonne did not give him enough finances to live on: in the beginning of his treatise he confessed that he wrote his work "for some young friends" who wanted an introduction to music (a type of *Musiklehre*), and who contributed, as he says, "a lot to his livelihood." This may indicate, too, that he didn't come from a very well-situated family, and it would explain, to some extent, why he was able to look with such an open mind at the social differences in the musical life of his time and place.

In addition to this, there must have been other and stronger impulses to do so. Although we have no direct information, one may guess that Grocheio, at least in his way of thinking, belonged to a progressive line within scholastic thought: the so-call Franciscan Nominalism (initiated formerly by Roger Bacon), which had one of its most important centers in Paris. Within this direction of medieval philosophy, based on experience, cognition, and mathematics, the sophisticated dialectics, the meaning of church authorities with a long written tradition in dogmatic books which dominated in the conservative camp of scholastics no longer had influence; but instead, facts and sources, the immediate experience with reality, nature and society, took precedence. The works of Aristotle, especially his writings on nature, were

Johannes de Grocheio (Facsimile Edition, Leipzig, 1972) and Johannes Wolf in SIMG I (1899–1900), 65–130, which is the first translation of the text.

studied extensively. All kinds of factual information were proven, including facts about the Near and Far East (brought to the European continent by tradesmen and travelers like Marco Polo), all of which broadened the horizon of knowledge. It was like an explosion of new information waiting to be incorporated into a new system of thinking. And it was upon this totally new foundation for knowledge that, in the early fourteenth century, the new natural science of the Parisian research center around Wilhelm von Ockham could grow in a really modern sense within a circle of scientists, among them physicists and mathematicians such as Albert von Sachsen and Nikolaus von Oresme, and—not to forget—the astronomer, mathematician and musical theorist Johannes de Muris.

This is the background of Grocheio's treatise which Heinrich Besseler has stated to be

> the most original and most independent attempt to develop from the new world view: also a new perspective and general picture of music. . . . Educated by Aristotelian empiricism, Grocheio comprehends music as a social reality, or fact, and develops from this angle, by concentrating on his Parisian environment: for the first time a sociologically based system of musical forms.

From every part of his writing one feels the spirit of an "open-minded observer," whether it be regarding nature-related issues or societal facts and problems.

For Grocheio the different aspects of music seem to be a permanent stimulus to discuss his topic on several levels—the acoustical and physiological preconditions, its morphological features, its psychological effects, as well as its social implications. All of this enters into his general judgment, thus adding interdisciplinarity to his thinking and writing. And one should not be astonished that he realized and anticipated facts which only in the last two centuries could be studied and verified experimentally by the developing modern sciences (such as psycho-physics and sensual psychology). To give only one example, let us mention his statements on the human ability of auditory discrimination which he discusses within the context of the principles of time measurment and the explanation of the term *tempus:*

> This measure, the *tempus,* is divided by some [theorists] in two equal parts, by others in three, and so on, up to six. We, instead of this, say that it may be divided up to the infinite, because it participates in the principle of continuity. But since we talk here about instrumental and vocal sounds *(sonis et vocibus),* we say that it may be divided up to the point where the auditive sense is able to perceive a difference.

By taking into account the psycho-physical conditions of perception with respect to the division of the continuity of time, he arrives at correct observations about the limits of the human ear, or about the so-called discrimination thresholds with the human "field of hearing" (which also depend on the different kinds of acoustical stimulus: the "ability of temporal dissolution" *(zeitliches Auflösungsvermögen)* of the auditive sense that may be lower or higher due to different musical contexts).

This strongly empirical attitude of Grocheio holds true also for his societal analysis of music. At first he mentions a fact which at his time no music theorist would have bothered with, namely that there were "several and different kinds of music, due to different customs, dialects, and languages within different states and regions:"

> *Partes autem musicae plures sunt et diversae secundum diversos usus, diversa idiomata, vel diversas linguas in civitatibus vel regionibus diversis.*

Just this would make it so difficult, he says, to arrive at a sufficient classification. And it is, therefore, that he concentrates on that part of the music of his time which he knows best: that is, the music in Paris and its surroundings (which means, in the most progressive center of arts and scholastic learning during the high Middle Ages, thinking that this advanced musical practice, also because of its thorough study by theorists, could very well serve as an example).

The kinds and types of music found in and around Paris are classified by the author into three main groups, which are differentiated in principle (without neglecting existing relations and connections). The first class is made up of the *musica simplex vel civilis, quam musicam vulgarem appellamus* which we will discuss in more detail presently. In the second class we meet the *musica composita vel regularis vel canonica, quam appellant musicam mensuratam,* that is, the (partly newly invented) vocal polyphony (such as the *organum,* the *conductus* and the *motetus),* a music for educated people and experts, separated more and more from church contexts, for which a new *ars scribendi* had to be developed: the mensural notation.

Finally, the third class contains the *musica ecclesiastica,* which does not simply mean church music, but its heart: the liturgical music. (Paraliturgical genres are excluded.) It is—*cum grano salis*—made up of the other two classes of music (*ex istis duobus efficitur*), and it "preserves" (in the sense of Hegel) their features (*ad melius ordinantur*).

We will not follow the classification process here in detail, but only mention that the description of the first two classes by several adjectives played an important role in this process. These attributes are related to each other in a systematic way, so that *composita* and *simplex* on the one hand and *regularis vel canonica* and *civilis* on the other will explain each other under certain circumstances.

The three basic categories of music are described by Grocheio under the following viewpoints:

- social and cultural functions
- performers (singers, musicians), listeners and authors
- contents (mainly in vocal music)
- effects (those intended and those which may be observed)
- musical features in a narrower sense: character of expression, tempo, performing style, tonal structure, types of forms (kind, number and order of parts, general designation)
- compositional process and notation
- musical and aesthetic valuation (*Werturteil*)

Concerning existing relations between the three classes of music in form, style and compositional type, Grocheio includes examples for cross-social processes of adaptation which are so typical for Western Europe in this progressive period of music history, and which makes it more likely that parts and ideas of it could travel a century later to other parts of the world.

Concentrating on *musica vulgaris,* we would like to know, primarily, the proper meanings of the term *vulgaris* and its defining circumscriptions *simplex* and *civilis.* How should we translate them? As folk music? Popular music (*Populärmusik*, also: *volkstümliche Musik* [a term with differing meanings during the last two centuries])? Music for everyone (*Musik der Allgemeinheit*)? Ordinary, common, vulgar or everyday music? Secular music? Laymen's music? Music of uneducated people? Or what else?

Within the musicological literature on Grocheio, we may find the whole spectrum. And there are further circumscriptions which orientate primarily on *simplex* and *civilis,* such as *bürgerliche Musik,* or *weltliche Einstimmigkeit.* Heinrich Besseler (in *MGG,* within the article on *ars antiqua*) circumscribes it as *einstimmig-umgangsmässige Musik,* a term which does not try to translate, but attempts to bring together the contents of all of the adjectives. To me it seems more adequate than all of the other translations. But the kernel of what Grocheio tried to express is not captured here either.

Johannes Wolf and Ernst Rohloff, who produced the well-known editions of the Grocheio texts, translate *civilis* as *bürgerlich, vulgaris* as *volkstümlich* or *Volks-(musik),* but *simplex* as *einfach* (simple), and not as *einstimmig,* which seems preferable to me because *einstimmig* could be easily misunderstood as purely unisonal, which often does not function in popular and folk music contexts, not to mention instrumental accompaniment of song.[6]

Concerning *"volkstümlich"* (which Rohloff uses throughout his translation for *vulgaris),* one could present a whole lecture on changing meanings since the word was created in 1794, beginning with the sense "specific for a people," meaning "national." Later on "commonly understood" or "commonly accepted and liked" predominated, while in twentieth-century

---

[6] In 1900 and 1972, respectively (see note 3), with intermediate steps by Rohloff in 1925–1926 and 1943.

folk music research, particularly under the influence of the concept of "pure, old and authentic folk song," one finds negative implications of "bad taste," "sentimentality," "lacrimose," etc.

Among the details with the Grocheio text which could contribute to a better understanding of the term *musica vulgaris*, let us mention the following three: first, the narrow relationship between vocal and instrumental genres in his classification system which play an important role in the author's concept and build up a kind of key for an adequate interpretation; secondly, the problem of orality concerning the *vulgaris* traditions, or, more precisely, the fact that parts of these traditions are included for the first time into the written (notated) corpus in the thirteenth century, which would be a precondition for discussion by a theorist like Grocheio; and finally, the highly interesting problem of tonality in the *vulgaris* genres, where the rules of the church modes are not valid, or at least not obligatory. This may easily be checked by studying notations of troubadours and trouvère chansons (where, as well, *musica ficta* or *falsa* are problematic).

Concerning the genres and musical types of *musica vulgaris*, Grocheio discusses about eleven different items. Two of them are mentioned more casually, but are, nevertheless, important to be familiar with. The genres are classified into three groups, as shown in figure 1.

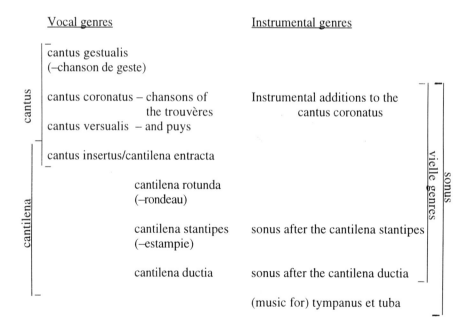

Fig. 1. *musica vulgaris*

Under "Vocal genres,", there are two groups of vocal music: above, the *cantus* forms without a refrain (beside the epic *cantus gestualis,* mainly the chansons of the trouvère and *puys*: *cantus coronatus* and *cantus versualis,* which is among others, used for educational purposes), and below, the *cantilena* forms with a refrain (the *rondeau,* the vocal *estampie,* and a dance-song type, called *ductia).* Between these two groups mediates a song type which may be *cantus* (without a refrain) or *cantilena* (with a refrain); but since Grocheio does not say much about it, one can only guess at what this type comprises.

Under "Instrumental genres," there are the instrumental pieces *(sonus):* the instrumental *estampie* and *ductia,* played on the *viella,* as well as the instrumental parts of the *cantus coronatus* (which may serve as *praeludium, interludium,* epilogue, or even accompaniment). There is also an interesting type of music for trumpets and timpani, used at festivals and tournaments, but again Grocheio does not say much about it. As the twofold use of *stantipes* and *ductia* indicates, Grocheio realizes a strong connection between vocal and instrumental genres. The same pieces of music may be either sung or played, as we know very well from folk music practice.

Of special interest are the different social classes involved in this kind of music. The performers may be highly appreciated artists such as Tassinus (a court musician), or masters of music and their advanced pupils/adepts in the *puys,* or professional minstrels, jongleurs and epic singers, or even young people in the countryside who perform the traditional repertory of their village. The listeners may consist of middle and lower class people, especially in the cities, of workers and old people, but they may come as well from noble families and dynasties. The music may be presented on stage (what Heinrich Besseler has called *Darbietungsmusik,* e.g., stage-audience-communication), as in the *cantus* types and *viella* genres; or it may also be an interactive type of musical communication (often within a social group, where everybody knows each other, e.g., *Umgangsmusik,* in the terminology of Besseler)[7] typical of the *cantilena* genres, which are partly used for dancing.

One must realize that *Musica vulgaris* is an extremely complex term, encompassing various kinds of music. This music includes the genres of municipal and rural folk music (the vocal *cantilena* forms), with the folklore of the cities dominating. Young people of both sexes from the Normandy region are mentioned only in connection with the *rondeau.* In Grocheio's time, these orally-transmitted refrain forms (which belong to the old strata of folk music in many cultures) began to spread from their original layers to the

---

[7] Heinrich Besseler, "Grundfragen des musikalischen Hörens" (1926) and "Das musikalische Hören der Neuzeit" (1956), both in *Aufsätze zur Musikästhetik und Musikgeschichte* (Leipzig, 1978), pp. 29–53 and 104–173. See also D. Stockmann, "Die ästhetisch-kommunikativen Funktionen der Musik unter historischen, genetischen und Entwicklungs-Aspekten," in *Beiträge zur Musikwissenschaft* 22 (Berlin, 1980), 126–144; "Musik und Sprache in intermodaler ästhetischer Kommunikation," in *Yearbook for Traditional Music* 13 (1981), 60–81; "Grundtypen musikalischer Kommunikation und ihre rezeptive Bewertung," in *Musikhören als Kommunikationsprozess* (Berlin, 1985), pp. 7–20.

middle and noble classes, including the expert circles of the *musica mensurata*. Within this process of cross-social adoption, they came in contact with written tradition and *ars notandi* for the first time.

Musica vulgaris also includes professionally presented genres such as the *cantus gestualis* which belongs to folklore in a wider sense, because it is handed down from singer to singer orally, and also because of its performance, structure, and content, but mainly because of its new sociological context. During the thirteenth century the old *chanson de geste*, created around 1100 within the feudal nobility (although apparently with deeper roots in tribal epic traditions of late antiquity, as mentioned, for example, by Boëthius), lost its former elite character and acquired totally new entertainment functions for lower- and middle-class people in the developing medieval cities. The representative signaling music for *tympanum et tuba*, as well as the *cantilena entrata*, or *cantus insertus*, which belonged to municipal as well as courtly life in those days, may also be categorized between popular and folk music: folklore in a wider sense.

There is a third group of songs which one may call popular of "volkstümlich" (in the second or third meaning mentioned above), as the *cantus versualis*, sometimes also called *cantilena*, which Grocheio does not value very highly; in any case, less than the *cantus coronatus*. Since it is used, among other things, for educational purposes, one may compare it with the category of didactic or school songs.

Finally, there are artistic genres of patrician and court music in *Musica vulgaris*, which also belong to the repertory of the bourgeois and intellectual *puys*. They were performed only by professional artists and trained musicians. Grocheio describes them as highly artistic and subtle genres of the new presentational art for privileged people and experts. Some of these pieces became very well known, but this should not be misunderstood to mean that they were popular with all classes of people.

Although the spectrum of Grocheio's *musica vulgaris* is rather broad, a good deal of the contemporary repertory outside the *musica ecclesiastica* and *mensurata* is, nevertheless, missing: no work songs, no laments, ritual songs or lullabies, no street calls, and no music of the herding people and peasants are mentioned. It is true that there are almost no documents of this kind of music from the thirteenth century, but one must suppose that they existed, as they did in antiquity. The main reason for Grocheio not mentioning those genres seems to be that they—being of no interest to educated people—were not adopted into the written culture, while the *rondeau* and the other *cantilena* types were, as was the *cantus gestualis*, at least partly, concerning the texts. This would also explain why the contemporary repertory of the *Spielleute*— who did not belong to the highly appreciated group of *viella* experts—is missing; it took centuries for this kind of music to be notated.

But there is one medieval vocal genre not mentioned by Grocheio which entered written tradition, at least partly and through the back door: the non-Latin spiritual song of paraliturgical character. It began to flourish in middle and western Europe; not so much in France, but within the German-speaking areas and in middle and northern Italy, as well as on the Iberian peninsula—the songs of the flagellants *(Geisslerlieder),* pilgrim songs, and the Italian laude, but neither Grocheio nor Dante say a word about them. One does not know the reason why, but it is known that as late as 1424–25, Pope Johannes XXII in his *Constitutio docta sanctorum* made a strong front against *triplis et motetibus vulgaribus.* And some earlier ecclesiastical sources, including French ones, do the same. So one can imagine that a man employed at a theological college, as Grocheio was, would shrink from setting up propaganda for an unofficial kind of spiritual music.

Keeping in mind what is missing (which would support a better understanding of the intellectual situation among educated people around 1300), how could one describe this *musica simplex vel civilis,* or *musica vulgaris?* In my opinion, it is first a simple music *(simplex)* insofar as it does not necessarily need notation, at least not in the same sense as the *musica mensurata* which would not exist without notation. *Simplex* is the classificatory opposite to *composita* (composed, put together), and it may be interpreted as *non composita,* but not necessarily single-voiced, or unison, since it may have been sung in groups (perhaps with heterophonic or even harmonic elements), or with instrumental accompaniment. Second, it is indigenous *(einheimische,* non-Latin) music; this is one of the Middle Latin meanings of *civilis* (never used by musicologists who translated or wrote about Grocheio). While the *musica mensurata vel canonica vel regulata* had its origin within the Latin ecclesiastical tradition (including certain kinds of rules) and developed a new set of strict rules for polyphonic composition, the *musica civilis* is based on French folk traditions which do not follow such stringent rules. But, by cross-cultural adaptation, it has become something different, too—it is no longer folk music in a strict sense. Finally, concerning *vulgaris,* Grocheio will say that this music is not connected with the Latin, but with the peoples' language, namely Old French (the *langue d'oil* which around 1300 started to push aside the other dialects, e.g., the Picardic). *Volkssprachlich, Muttersprachlich* and *nationalsprachlich* are well-known Middle Latin meanings of the term *vulgaris,* which—strangely enough—have never been used in the musicological literature on Grocheio either. The obstacle here was obviously that Grocheio included instrumental genres within his *vulgaris* concept.

Musica simplex vel civilis vel vulgaris may have secular or spiritual character (in the same manner as the *musica mensurata,* in which *vulgaris* elements are included here and there). Socially it may belong to several classes, and the singers and musicians may be laymen, professionals or highly decorated artists. Thus, this music is neither folk music nor popular music (in any special sense whatsoever), nor *bürgerliche* nor court music, but it includes the whole gamut in a new way, ranging from a simple rural dance song to a subtle trouvère chanson, from the musically unpretentious epic narration in the market place in front of an anonymous audience of mostly lower class people to a highly artistic *estampie* improvisation by an *artifex in viella* in front of kings and noblemen.

Musica vulgaris, as Grocheio described it, is the result of a new type of cross-social adaptation and exchange, and part of a progressive cultural process, that had a strong tendency to connect or unite all kinds of people in French society (regardless of the social layers they belonged to), i.e., citizens of the country who spoke the same tongue. Grocheio as well as Dante were fighting, each of them in his own country and in his own special way, against the *lateinische Bildungswelt,* "the Latinized world," and for the official acceptance of their mother tongues in poetry, which would, much earlier than in other parts of the world, create the basis for the development of a national consciousness and feeling of national identity.

But Grocheio's *musica vulgaris* is not only based on a common language, but also on a common musical heritage which is bound to this language. For this musical heritage, the national idiom of the Ile-de-France, the Old French, may have been a fundamental generative factor. Not only the linguistic and poetic structure of the texts, but also the intonation patterns of the melodies may have been influenced by it, including way of performing, the rhythmic structuring, etc. This could explain, at least to some extent, why Grocheio had no problems in subordinating purely instrumental genres under the keyword *vulgaris:* in his opinion, they participated in the typically French "musical gesture" *(Gestus).*

Thus one may say that *musica vulgaris* as a whole is based on indigenous musical traditions (which continued to exist in French folk music for centuries to come), but during the thirteenth century, this music developed into a common French musical idiom, created by different genres and forms which are no longer pure folk music. These forms include the popular refrain forms (the *rondeaux, virelais, ballades);* the genres of the trouvère's art; the non-Latin spiritual song of epic or lyric character, such as the legend-like types of the *cantus gestualis* (which lost the functions of the old *chanson de geste,* but survives in the repertories of professional narrators, telling the old stories for a new municipal audience, and which became the starting point for the development of a new type of folklore genre: the narrative spiritual song, the folk ballads, and romances); and the new instrumental genres, from the representative *Geleit- und Einzugsmusiken,* and the signaling forms up to the instrumental dances and presentational pieces for pure listening, the *ductiae, estampies* and *notae.*

It is mainly by these instrumental forms—and the *musica mensurata,* of course—that a new epoch of presentational music-making started, performed only for passive enjoyment. But written collections of instrumental music only very slowly came into being.

Eventually most of the genres of *musica vulgaris,* insofar as they did not yet exist outside of France, crossed national borderlines into Spain and Portugal, Britain, Germany, Italy, etc. In Dante's *De vulgari eloquentia,* for example, well-known French *vulgaris* examples are quoted. But on the other hand, although the process described here had its center in France, there seem to have been, from the very beginning, influences from the outside, e.g., concerning the *virelais* (which Grocheio does not mention *expressis verbis),* obviously from Spain. The same may be true, at least to some extent, for the *cantus gestualis,* as epic narration, the *cantares de gesta,* were common among the Spanish *juglares* since the times of the *reconquista;* and it was even in Spain that the romance style developed (which in the fourteenth century became folk poetry, performed mainly by beggars and blind musicians). There is also, by the way, a Spanish folksong type for courting, called *ronda,* but unfortunately sources from the older times are not as eloquent as we would like them to be.[8]

Thus, concerning the mediation of one or the other genre of *music vulgaris* to other continents during the period of colonization and Christianization from the end of the fifteenth century onwards, one can not deny that some preconditions for this kind of export existed. Men of flesh and blood were traveling to the New World, including musicians with their home repertory in mind, as they had been traveling over all of Europe, from Germany and the Netherlands to Spain, from France to Britain or Italy, mediating parts of their repertories from country to country and bringing home new music that they learned abroad. Why not expect that this common practice (although difficult to trace) would occur in other parts of the world?

Finally, let us look at some examples, and in so doing, keep in mind that there are not only *vulgaris* genres, but also conceptual aspects of *musica vulgaris*—as a means of becoming aware of national or regional identity throughout the different groups and classes of a society under the conditions of foreign control in language and culture—which could be of some importance to colonized and proselytized countries.

Among folklorists it is rather well known that the colonial areas of the romance language countries, especially of France, Portugal and Spain (including the Catalonian and Provençal dialects), are important for different kinds of research into the history of genres because of the relative antiquity of their traditions.[9] Mentioned by Erich Seeman are, for example, Canada for French folklore and northern Africa for Spanish folklore. The romance of the Spanish province Castille which came into being in the early Middle Ages but which had its roots, according to Seeman, in the epic tradition of the *chanson de geste,*[10] or, as I would guess, in the changed form of the *cantus gestualis* often found its special subject matter in the struggles against the North African Moors *(Mauren).* The Spanish romance, with its eight-syllable lines and four-line stanzas also spread throughout Latin America during the centuries after the initial Spanish settlement, and there one may find well-preserved forms, as well as those with considerable variation and structural change.

---

[8] See for example the following articles in MGG: Marius Schneider, "Spanien," Vol. 12; João de Freitas Branco, "Portugal," Vol. 10; Mario de Sampayo Ribeiro, "Lissabon," Vol. 8.

[9] Erich Seeman, "Die europäische Volksballade," *Handbuch des Volksliedes* I, ed. Wilhelm Brednich, Lutz Röhrich, and Wolfgang Suppan (Munich, 1973), 37–56.

[10] Seeman, "Die europäische Volksballade," p. 41.

The Caribbean islands were either settled by the French, or were in some way the object of French influence. From Grenada, Haiti, Cuba and Trinidad, we know about genres such as the *juba,* the *bele (bel air)* and the *calenda,* all dance songs. These songs were generally started by a solo singer, followed by the chorus and the refrain (and, additionally, by a drum part, stemming from an African heritage), the words of which are sung in the Old French *patois,* known in Grenada as "broken French." Here one would have to prove in more detail connections discovered with older French dance layers and refrain forms. Even concerning the so-called *tuma françesca* and the *quadrilles* of the nineteenth century, direct proof of their origins is by no means easy.

As another example of Spanish influence, one could mention the Philippines, discovered in 1521 by Magalhães (who died there), but in the last decades of that century (after 1560) settled by the Spaniols and named after Philip II (in 1543). There are four genres of Philippine music which have their basis in the Spanish colonial period (c. 1600–1898): the *banda,* the *rondalla,* the *kundiman,* and the *sarswela.*[11] The latter is a kind of popular musical theatre (a follower of the Spanish *Zarzuela,* created by Caldéron), while the *kundiman* (a kind of national art song comparable to the French *chanson* and the German *Lied*) derived its name from an earlier folk genre: an improvised dance song on frustrated or unrequited love. But, by the time the composed *kundiman* appeared, the folk genre was already extinct, apparently going into decline in the early nineteenth century.

Concerning the *rondella,* a plucked string ensemble which derives its general characteristics and name from Hispanic sources, both European and New World: it is the name which is striking after our discussion of *musica vulgaris.* Although the *rondellus,* or, as Grocheio says, *rotundellus,* is a vocally-performed refrain genre, the old name may indicate deep-rooted relationships. Change from vocal to instrumental performance, as we said earlier, could easily have taken place. What is interesting, is that (with the exception of the guitar) all *rondalla*-plucked lutes underwent further evolution in the Philippines, contrasting in construction with their Spanish and Mexican counterparts. But the musical style is Hispanic, with simple triadic harmony and shifts between major and minor modes without modulation. The basis for the repertory are popular nineteenth-century rhythms—the *paso doble,* the polka, the waltz, the march, and the *habañera.* While its earliest use in the Philippines, like its Spanish counterpart (known variously as *rondalla, cumparsa* or *estudiantina)* was for serenade and dance accompaniment, the ensemble was gradually adapted to other uses, such as competitions, concerts and school music. At present, it is regarded by Filipinos as the most typically Filipino instrumental music ensemble and is prominent in cultural missions, official receptions, and celebrations of national significance, thus functioning

---

[11] Ricardo D. Trimillos, "Tradition and colonialism in the Philippines: a diachronic phenomenon," in *Tradition in den Musikkulturen: Heute und Morgen, Bericht über die wissenschaftliche Konferenz des Internationalen Musikrates 1985* (Leipzig, 1987), pp. 108–116.

as a cultural emblem—a concept which seems comparable to that of the old *musica vulgaris.*

Also interesting is the *banda,* or wind band, which is reminiscent of the open-air music for *tympanum et tuba.* As Trimillos points out, it is

> the only one of the four Philippine genres that maintains a clear parallel to its Spanish counterpart. It was used by the Spanish establishment both for secular (governmental) occasions as well as religious ones. The present musical style . . . is surprisingly similar to that of town wind bands of Spain and Mexico.[12]

The *bandas* are indispensable to local celebrations, and during the colonial period they were apparently sponsored either by the diocese, or by the town government. During the American-influenced period (after 1898), the wind bands received positive reinforcement by the military band, but the Spanish *banda* and the American bands, nevertheless, represented two separate streams of wind band music in the Philippines, the former providing a locus for regional identity. The *serenata* competition of two *bandas* from different towns reminds us of the competitions within the old *puys* (where the *cantus coronatus,* the crowned chanson, was the winner).

To give a last example, let us turn to a Portuguese-influenced country of Latin America: Brazil, which from 1500 to 1822 belonged to Portugal. Just as the Hispanic, the old Galician-Portuguese musical culture (from the twelfth to fourteenth centuries) included poetry and musical practice of troubadours and trouvères, as well as instrumentalists *(Spielleute).* The book paintings in the preserved *cancioneiros* remind us of the well-known Spanish paintings from the Castilian court of Alfonso the Wise. Source material before the eighteenth century is hardly extant (because of several earthquakes), and therefore the musical traditions of the colonies attained considerable importance.

Scholars doing research in these traditions have recently pointed out that categorical differences between art music, popular and folk music did not exist among the Portuguese people in Brazil.[13] This reminds us again of the medieval *vulgaris* concept. Mostly a mixture of stylized folk music, music for entertainment and art music was used in everyday life, or during celebrations. Narrative folk poetry which could be recited, sung or expressed with mimics and gestures mediated medieval epics and *Lebensgefühl* into the new homelands, among them the legend of *König Karl* (which Grocheio mentions among the topics of *cantus gestualis),* the fights of the crusaders, conflicts between the Christian and Muslim worlds, the adventures of the discovery and colonizing period, etc. Romances, which may also contain elements of the

---

[12] Trimillos, "Tradition and colonization in the Philippines," p. 110.

[13] Antonio Alexandre Bispo, "Das abendländische Musikerbe portugiesischer Prägung," in *Brasilien, Einführung in Musiktraditionen Brasiliens,* ed. Tiago de Oliveira Pinto (Mainz, 1986), pp. 58–76.

medieval *cantigas (de amor, de amigo, de escárnio, de mal-dizer),* have been transmitted from the old to the new homelands. Of special interest are the so-called *cucuru* in the region of São Paulo, which are meetings of *trovadores*—singers who improvise texts by competing with each other, mostly in pairs.[14] In the midwest *(Mato Grosso),* ten to twelve singers perform in the singing competition, which always takes place in front of an audience and which is accompanied by two *violas* (guitars) and a *pandeiro* (tambourine). This *cucuru* in the southeast and midwest of Brazil is a modern, culturally adapted version of the poetic and musical competitions of the Provençal troubadours of the eleventh and twelfth centuries (which developed into a somewhat modernized form in the municipal *puys* of Grocheio's time). Up to now it is not known how this special musical performance came to Brazil, but it is known that branches of this practice existed and still exist in Portugal *(escola provençal).* The *trovadores* sing on religious, satirical and other topics *(Spiellieder),* as the old troubadours did, and partly revived old functions within special ceremonies. They also educate *canturinos* (apprentices), a medieval tradition as well. In general, the *trovadores* are literate enough to study the Bible, the legend of King Karl, and other things such as medieval heroic legends.

Even a patron or protector of a woman or man is known on the basis of *Minne,* friendship, or special interest in a singer, a custom which generates songs of thanks and praise (similar to the Provençal *sirventes).* Within these songs, the "house" becomes a "castle," the audience is thought to be feudal, belonging to a "court," and so forth. In performance the *trovadore* seems to be, as Julieta de Andrade has written, a mixture of a medieval *troubadour,* a *jongleur* and a *Spielmann;* a special combination which obviously does not go out of fashion, but may find its audience even today in many parts of the world.

INTERNATIONAL COUNCIL FOR TRADITIONAL MUSIC, GERMANY

---

[14] Julieta de Andrade, "Cucuru: Liebesdichtung und Epengesang in São Paulo," in *Brasilien,* pp. 77–87.

Bipolarity and the Fifth Interval in Gamelan and Medieval European Music

by José Maceda

A cursory review of bipolarity and the fifth interval in the European Middle Ages is intended only to show how the two are differently used in the gamelan. Gregorian and Ambrosian chants which anteceded the use of two and three voices had ending tones or tonics, but no single dominant or opposing tone that led to the tonic. The opposing tone which is the fifth degree, or dominant, came about as an historical process, a technique of bipolarity, that became clearer in the sixteenth and seventeenth centuries through the use of harmony and after the discovery of equal temperament.

Examination of a few examples in Willi Apel's *Historical Anthology of Music* would suffice to illustrate these two elements of bipolarity and the fifth interval. Early organum with parallel octaves, fifths and fourths (Ex. 25) merely followed the *vox principalis,* with no special significance in their placements in the vocal line. Bipolarity was totally absent then. In Leoninus' organum (Ex. 29), more use of unisons, fifths and other intervals shows an exploration of their possibilities, of how to place fifths vis-à-vis the octave or the unison as ending tone without showing a clear relationship between these intervals.

In the motet *Hec Dies* (Ex. 32), shown as figure 1, there is some direction in the use of fifth intervals. In the tenor, the first phrase *a, g, b-flat, a* ends with a fifth above *a.* The second phrase, *g, a, f, a,* ends with a unison on *a'* above. There is an opposition, a bipolarity between the fifth of the first phrase and the unison of the second. The latter unison is deemed as ending the two phrases, and the former fifth is a point of preparation, an antecedent to the consequent ending tone. In the fifth interval, the note *e'* is a fifth above its lower voice *a.*

Fig. 1. *Hec Dies*[1]

---

[1] Willi Apel and Archibald Davison, *Historical Anthology of Music,* 2 vols. (Cambridge, 1950), I:32.

In figure 2, the *virelai Plus dure* by Guillame de Machaut (Ex. 46b), there is a further search for the use of the fifth degree. In measures one through four, the fifths are placed on *g* and *f* of the tenor; a sixth is on *e;* and an octave on *d,* the ending tone of this phrase. This succession of two fifths and a sixth is a preparation for the ending with an octave on *d,* the tonic. The sixth with a *c''-sharp* acts as the dominant, the pole that leads to that tonic. Similarly, the phrase from mm. 5–9 is led to end on tonic *d* in m. 9 by the use of leading tones *c'-sharp* and *c''.*

The use of that *c'-sharp* is repeated in mm. 21, 32 and 34. In other words, a technique of bipolarity that isolates the tonic through the use of a dominant had only its beginnings in *Plus dure.* Here, the leading tone acts as a bipolar tone.

Fig. 2. Guillaume de Machaut, *Plus dure*[2]

In figure 3, Dufay's *Mon chier amy* (Ex. 67) written in the 15th century, exhibits fifth degrees leading to their ending tones. These are shown in measures three and four between tones *e* in the contratenor and *a* in the tenor where *a* is the ending tone for this phrase, and also in measures nine and ten between tones *a* and *d*, where *d* is a deceptive ending tone; and in mm. 12, 13 and 14 between tones *d*, *g* and *a*, where *d* is the ending tone or tonic.

---

[2] Ibid., I:49.

Fig. 3. Guillaume Dufay, *Mon chier amy*[3]

[3] Ibid., I:73.

These few examples point out how the isolation of the fifth degree of the scale through a technique of bipolarity came about as a slow historical process. Polyphony through the use of two and three voices brought about vertical intervals which had to be disciplined. The controlling factor is the ending tone or tonic, and the historical process emphasized that tone through a technique of bipolarity. The bipolar tone, the fifth interval of the tonic became more clearly identified in various cadences of the seventeenth and eighteenth centuries.[4]

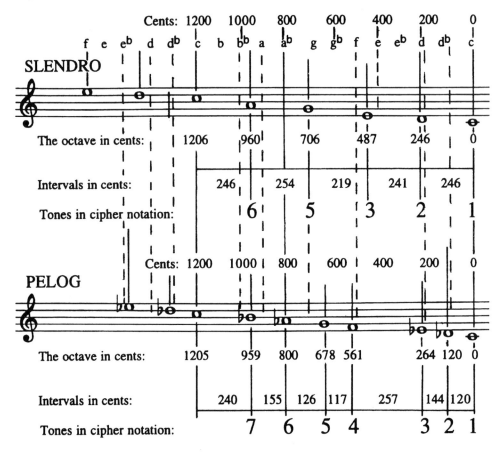

Fig. 4. Slendro and Pelog scales[5]

---

[4] *Harvard Dictionary of Music,* ed. Willi Apel (Cambridge, 1972), pp. 118–121; *The New Grove Dictionary of Music and Musicians,* ed. Stanley Sadie (London, 1980), 3:582–586.
[5] Cents after Mantle Hood, "Slendro and Pelog Redefined," *Selected Reports* (1966), 45–vi, iii.

In the Javanese gamelan, a thoroughly different musical situation prevails. Instead of diatonic melodies and a structure of tetrachords, the background is a musical world based on pentatonic structures which are generally applied in East and Southeast Asia, in both court and folk musics. The presence of dual pentatonic scales in Southeast Asia—*slendro* and *pelog* in Java, *kulilal* and *bagit* plus *binalig* and *dinaladay* in the Philippines, and similar half-steps in *bac* and *nam* in Vietnam, in *ryo-ritsu* and two scales in *Noh* in Japan—point to a theory and practice of dual scales in Southeast Asia as a possible source of origin, different from a theory of a cycle of fifths in China (Maceda 1990).[6]

In the Javanese gamelan *slendro* is made up of anhemitonic steps while *pelog* uses half-steps (see figure 4). The tunings vary in all gamelan but an example of a tuning measured by a Stroboconn would highlight the difference between the two scales. In *pelog*, although there are seven tones, only five tones are used at a time.

Melodies constructed on these scales rely on traditional cadential formulae and ending tones which identify the character of the music or its *pathet*. The following are the traditional cadential formulae. The preferred ending tones are underlined. In the music itself, there is a great variation in the application of these formulae and in the programming of ending or *Gongan* tones. These formulae may be inverted, or only parts of it may be played.

Slendro Pathet [7]

Nem (avoids 1)	653<u>2</u>		216 <u>5</u>
Sanga (avoids 3)	216<u>5</u>		53<u>2</u>(1)
Manyura (avoids 5)	321<u>6</u>		65<u>3</u>(2)

Pelog Pathet
Lima (avoids 7)	5(4)32<u>1</u>		216 <u>5</u>
Nem (avoids 4)	216(<u>5</u>)		653 <u>2</u>
Barang (avoids 1,4)	327 <u>6</u>		653(<u>2</u>)

Of the five utilized tones in *pelog and slendro,* one is avoided or used less frequently. In effect, there remain only four tones that are played in the music of all *pathet.* These four tones are related to each other by the fifth degree or its inversion, the fourth. For example, in the cadence 6532, 2 is a fifth of 5; 6 is a fifth of 2; 3 is a fifth of 6. This fifth relationship applies as well to other cadential formulae illustrated above. In the *slendro pathet sanga* cadence 532(1), tone 3 is two fifths away from tone 2. Tone 3 is similarly related to tone 2 in *pelog pathet lima,* while in *slendro pathet manyura,* tone 1 takes the place of 7 as the fifth of 3 in the cadence 3216.

---

6 José Maceda, "In Search of a Source of Pentatonic Hemitonic and Anhemitonic Scales in Southeast Asia," *Acta Musicologica* II (1990), 192–223.

7 Mantle Hood, *The Evolution of Javanese Gamelan: Book III: Paragon of the Roaring Sea* (Wilhelmshaven, 1989), pp. 39–58.

In the foregoing, all five tones in *slendro* and five tones at a time in *pelog* are root structures, where each tone has equal weight or importance in relation to each other. With the pentatonic structure and relation of fifths to each other, an application of two musical techniques—"bipolarity" and "counts-of-four"—gives a sense of direction—a musical organization—to this structure.

Counts-of-four are a basic musical structure found not only in Javanese and Balinese gamelan but also in many other ensembles in Southeast Asia. The music of ensembles of flat gongs in the Philippines and Vietnam rely on counts of two or four. The counting is equally applied to music ensembles in the Malay peninsula, e.g., *Wayang Kulit, Nobat, Ma-yong, Main putri,* and in North Sumatra among the Batak and Acheh gong and drum ensembles; in village folk music of Java, *santolyo* and *gamelan reyog,* in the music of suspended gongs (*agung*) and gongs in a row (*kulintang*) in Mindanao, Borneo, and Thailand, and in rural ensembles of drum music in northern and northeast Thailand (Maceda 1986).[8] Four gongs were used as an altar to offer gifts to spirits in a thanksgiving ritual in Mindanao.[9] In East Asia, a court music in China and Japan is based on counts of four.

In the realm of culture, the number "four" is a fundamental structure and is symbolized in the square. In the building of a Hindu temple, a basic step is "to form at first a small square with four bricks in the middle of the Aquikatra, then to enlarge this square to one of 16," etc. It is in this way too, that the various types of *Vastumandala* are enumerated in *Vastusastra* in a progressive series of 1, 2, 3, and 4 units square, etc., the most sacred being the plan of 64 squares, preserving the meaning of 64 which is exemplified in 64 bricks from the spokes of the wheel, 64 of the *Veda*.[10]

Similarly, the square structure of Buddhist temples in Burma, Thailand and particularly the Borobudur in Java, is a prime example of the importance of counts-of-four. In the Borobudur, the base measures exactly 113 meters on each side.[11] The body of the temple consists of five square terraces, diminishing in size, while the top is made up of narrowing circular terraces.[12]

All these examples show how the number four is applied not only in folk and court musics of Asia, but also as a symbol in the construction of Hindu and Buddhist temples. In gamelan, it is heard as square proportions of counting, and in architecture the squareness is actually seen. A symbolism of the number four opens other numbers in music to other cosmological interpretations. Counts-of-four, bipolarity and the fifth interval may now be applied in actual musical examples in gamelan.

---

[8] José Maceda, "A Concept of Time in a Music of Southeast Asia," *Ethnomusicology* 30:11–53.

[9] Laura W. Benedict, "A Study of Bagobo Ceremonial: Magic and Myth," *Annals of the New York Academy of Sciences,* 25 (1916):125–126.

[10] Stella Kamrisch, *The Hindu Temple* (Calcutta, 1946), p.27.

[11] Soekmono, *Chandi Borodudur* (Paris, 1976), p.15.

[12] *Encyclopaedia Britannica* (1974), 17:267.

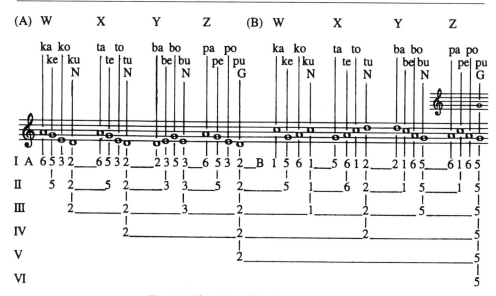

Fig. 5. *Udan Mas.* Slendro pathet nem.
Cadential formula: 6532; 2165 (Avoids 1)

In *Udan Mas* (see figure 5), counts-of-four are illustrated in phrases of four counts in Row I. In these counts—1, 2, 3, 4—the fourth counts under syllables *ku, tu, bu,* and *pu* are given more importance than their preceding numbers. Tone 2 under AWku is also the ending tone of 6532, the cadential formula that characterizes *slendro pathet nem.* Fourth counts under syllables AWku, Xtu, Ybu, Zpu emphasize respectively tones 2, 2, 3, 2 which may also be seen in Row III. These tones are stressed further by the *Kenong (N)* which plays these tones on their assigned beats, at the fourth of every count. In Row B, the fourth tones under syllables Wku, Xtu, Ybu, Zpu are respectively, 1, 2, 5, 5 as seen in Row III.

With counts-of-four goes also the element of bipolarity, of opposing two notes against each other. In Row IA, column W, this occurs between counts 1 and 2 *(ka and ke)* and 3 and 4 *(ko and ku).* The more important pole is on the second count *ke* with tone 5 and *ku* with tone 2. These tones carry more weight, a hierarchical position of command that helps define preferred tones in 6532 of the cadential formula, thus identifying the character of *slendro pathet nem.*

Still in Row I, the next bipolarity may be seen in column X where, under bipolar pairs *ta-te* and *to-tu,* the more important tones are those under *te* and *tu,* or 5 and 2 respectively. Further in Row IA, columns Y and Z follow the same order of bipolarity as do columns W, X, Y, and Z in row IB.

In Row IIA, the bipolar tones are now under WKe and Ku; Xte and tu; Ybe and bu; Zpe and pu. Similarly in Row IIB, this bipolar opposition follows.

In Row III, tones under Xtu are more important than those under WKu; likewise for Zpu and Ybu; and the rest of Row III. Rows IV and V show more oppositions in hierarchical fashion, and Row VI has only tone 5, the last in the hierarchy.

Row V contains two ending tones, 2 and 5, which are *Gongan* tones under AZpu and BZpu respectively. They are of equal importance, and, along with the different bipolar tones that led to this isolation, make up a whole logic that defines *Udan Mas* and describes its *pathet*.

Now for the fifth interval. It was said previously how all five tones in *slendro* and five tones at a time in *pelog* are each a fifth of each other. Without bipolarity and counts of four, they are of equal importance, with no one tone having more weight than the other. Counts-of-four and bipolarity isolate certain tones and put them in prominence. In Row I, bipolar tones 6–5 are separated by an interval of two fifths, and likewise in tones 3–2. Under column Y, tones 2–3 are also separated by two fifths, and between tones 5–3 by three fifths. Each of the pairs that follow are separated by two or more fifths.

In Row II, all pairs of tones are separated only by one interval of a fifth, except the pair 3–3. In *Udan Mas* the hierarchy of tones chosen by its music favors fifths that are one rather than several fifths removed from each other. This one fifth-interval relationship prevails in other *gendhing (Karawitan, Remeng, Kemban Mara,* and *Gendhing Tedjanata)* in Rows II, III and IV, but they are not always consistent. A direct fifth relationship in Row I of *Udan Mas* is only one of several ways of relating fifth intervals to each other. In these relationships, the weaker pole of bipolar tones has a preparatory role which, together with its stronger pole, may together carry different designations: weak-strong, antecedent-consequent, dissonance-consonance, preparation-resolution. The number of fifth intervals that separate two poles from each other seem to matter less than that the stronger pole marks the tones that identify the cadential formula of the *pathet*.

In *Udan* Mas, the most important ending tones which fall on the stroke of the big *Gongan* (*G*) on the sixteenth counts are tones 2 and 5 under AZpu and BZpu. They are the ending tones of the cadential formulae 653$\underline{2}$ and 216$\underline{5}$ that identify *slendro pathet nem*. They are a fifth apart and may be seen in level V of the music example.

A structure of counts-of-four, bipolarity and the fifth interval has a sense of logic that works like a syllogism with four rather than three statements. In *Udan Mas*, the first four statements in A—6532, 6532, 2353, 6532— terminates on the last statement 6532 with the tone 2. This last statement is a re-affirmation of the first two statements made more emphatic by the opposition of the third phrase 2353 which has a "contradictory," "dissonant" or "antecedent" quality. The next four statements in B are 1561, 5612, 2165, and 6165. They take up a completely different line, with ending tones on the fourth count being tones 1, 2, 5, 5 respectively and final *Gongan* on tone 5.

In gamelan logic and *Udan Mas*, it is perfectly admissible to have two endings, two *Gongan*, with different tones a fifth apart—tone 2 for the A statement and tone 5 for the B. However, if in the B statement, the fourth phrase turned out to be 6532, *Gongan* would be tone 2, and there would only be one tone for both statements. This ending on the same *Gongan* tone happens in other *gendhing—Ladrang Agun Agun, Gambir Sawit, Manik Maninten*—but endings on *Gongan* may have as many as five different tones. Two and one *Gongan* are the more common number of ending tones.

Hierarchy is outlined in figure 5 of *Udan Mas*. In Row I, all tones, members of the hierarchy, are present. Row II shows the elimination and isolation process. Tones 6 and 3 are less used, while tone 2 is emphasized. In Rows III, IV and V, the process of elimination is clear. As was pointed out previously, the choice of two or more ending or *Gongan* tones to identify a *pathet* or describe a cadential formula is what makes for an ambiguity in these ending tones. In effect, counts-of-four and bipolarity aim for ambiguity, although the mechanism they employ is precise.

PELOG

In *Pelog,* the use of half steps and a wide range of pitches between intervals do not affect bipolarity and the fifth interval, for these two elements are still the basic structure of those intervals. A piece of music, *Ladrang Sarilaja* in *pelog pathet lima,* may now be examined according to the role of these two elements of bipolarity and the fifth interval.

Ladrang is the stretched form of *lancaran* on which *Udan Mas* is based. In *ladrang,* there are eight tones or beats to a *Kenong* beat and four *Kenong* to one *Gongan,* a total of 32 tones or beats, instead of 16 in *lancaran* to make one *Gongan.* In effect, a musical phrase that takes eight tones instead of four to arrive at a point of emphasis on the *Kenong* would be delayed twice as much with a round-about way of arriving at the important point in *Kenong,* every eight beats, and in *Gongan* every 32 beats.

In figure 6, line 101, Row IV, the *Kenong* (N) tones are 2, 3, 2, and 5, with the last tone being *Gongan.* Each of these *Kenong* tones is surrounded, decorated by other tones in Rows I, II and III. In Row II, bipolarity between the second and fourth beats isolates tones 2, 2, 3, 3, shown in Row IIIA, and tones 1, 2, 1, 5, shown in Row IIIB. A similar isolation of tones in the fourth count may be seen in Row IV of lines 102 and 103.

Lines 101, 102 and 103 may be compared with each other. Lines 101 and 103 are similar; they complement each other. Tones in 103A are mostly a fifth above or related by a fifth to tones in 101A. Tones in 103B and 101B are the same.

The whole of line 102 may be taken as an intermediary between lines 101 and 103. In 102A, tone 1 acts in contrast to tone 2 in line 101A; tone 2 in line 102A contrasts with tone 3 in line 101A. Further, tone 6 in 102A contrasts with tone 5 in line 101A. In 102B at point Xtu, tone 6 is a fourth below tone 2 at the same point in line 101B above and line 103B below. Again, at point

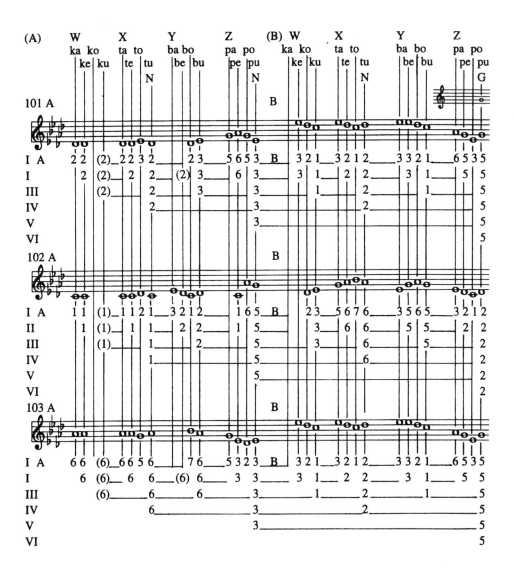

N. B. For truer pelog pitch, see figure 4.

Fig. 6. *Ladrang Sarilaja.* Pelog pathet lima.
Cadences: 5(4)32<u>1</u>; 216<u>5</u>; their inversions[13]

[13] Hood, *Paragon*, p. 316.

BYbu, tone 5 of 102B is a fourth of tone 1 in 101B and 103B. Finally, at point BZpu, tone 2 of 102B is a fourth below tone 5 in 101B and 103B. While 102A acts in contrast to 101A and 103A, 102B behaves as a bridge between 101B and 103B.

Altogether, lines 101, 102 and 103 are statements of logic where bipolarity and the fifth interval are the main tools of expression. Through these tools, words to express that logic, like complement, intermediary, contrast, and others used previously, show how bipolarity operates and how a structure of fifths is a convenient tool, the very interval that automatically opposes, complements, and contrasts one tone from another. Again, through the roles of opposition, contrast and complement, lines 101, 102 and 103 form a logic associated with Aristotelian causality. These may be stated as follows:

A	101A	a statement
	101B	its complement
B	102A	contrasting statement
	102B	contrasting complement
A1	103A	first statement modified
	104A	original complement

"A" consists of two parts: a statement and its complement. "B" is the contrasting statement and its complement. "A1" is the first statement modified and its complement, exactly the same as in "A."

Unlike a built-in relationship of fifth intervals in pentatonic scales, the fifth interval in Western music comes out of a tetrachord structure, and its function with the first degree of bipolar oppositions did not become clear until the seventeenth and eighteenth centuries, when harmonic progressions in sequences similar to statements in Aristotelian causality became a powerful tool of musical expression.

In the gamelan, the fifth interval is a built-in mechanism that facilitates bipolarity, but the ends of these tools are ambiguity and equivocation. The choices of ending of *Gongan* tones are limited, and it is in the process of choosing one or the other tone where equivocation arises. In "36 gendhing" of Dr. Mantle Hood's book, *Paragon of the Roaring Sea,*[14] a summary of the number of times that each tone 1, 2, 3, 4, 5, 6, 7 in both *slendro* and *pelog* is used as a *Gongan* tone follows:

---

[14] Ibid., pp. 304–327.

TONES:	1	(2)	3	4	(5)	6	7
PATHET:							
Slendro P. Nem	0	10	1	0	9	4	
Slendro P. Sanga	2	8	0	0	21	1	
Slendro P. Manyura	4	3	7	0	2	7	
Pelog P. Lima		7	3	5	0	15	5
Pelog P. Nem		1	10	3	0	10	3
Pelog P. Barang	0	7	3	0	3	12	6
TOTAL:	14	(41)	19	0	(60)	32	6

Fig. 7. Number of times each tone is used as *Gongan* in "36 Gendhing"[15]

Tone 4 is not used at all. Tones 5 and 2 are the preferred *Gongan* tones with 60 and 41 counts respectively, and with tone 6 coming up as a third preferred tone with 32 counts. Although 36 is only a small portion of hundreds or thousands of other *gendhing,* the table is an indication of a certain preference for these two tones.

Another table, figure 8, shows the preferred tones used as *Gongan* in each *pathet.* The *pathet* that uses mostly tones 2 and 5 are *slendro pathet nem* with 10 and 9 counts respectively, *slendro pathet sanga* with 8 and 21 counts, and *pelog pathet nem* with 10 counts each. *Pelog pathet lima* used tone 5 fifteen times. *Slendro pathet manyura* preferred tones 3 and 6 and *pelog pathet barang* preferred tones 2 and 6.

TONES:	1	2	3	5	6
			Number of times used:		
PATHET:					
Slendro P. Nem		10		9	
Slendro P. Sanga		8		21	
Slendro P. Manyura			7		7
Pelog P. Lima	7			15	
Pelog P. Nem		10		10	
Pelog P. Barang		7			12

Fig. 8. Preferred tones used as *Gongan* in each *pathet*

---

[15] Ibid., pp. 304–327.

Ending in *Gongan* tones may now be viewed according to the number of times they are used in twelve cadences of six *pathet*. These cadences are

Slendro P. Nem	216<u>5</u>	653<u>2</u>	
Slendro P. Sanga	216<u>5</u>	53<u>2</u>1	
Slendro P. Manyura		653<u>2</u>	321<u>6</u>
Pelog P. Lima	216<u>5</u>	5(4)3<u>2</u>1	
Pelog P. Nem	216<u>5</u>	653<u>2</u>	
Pelog P. Barang		653<u>2</u>	327<u>6</u>

Above, it can easily be seen how ending tones 5 and 2 are used more than tones 1 and 6. In actuality, there are many more variations of cadences and *Gongan* tones than those suggested by the formulae shown in figure 9.

In this figure, *slendro pathet nem* has *Gongan* endings on tones 2 and 5 in cadences 653<u>2</u> and 216<u>5</u> respectively. Other *Gongan* tones are tone 6 in *Ladrang Karawitan*, and tones 6 and 3 in *Ladrang Remeng*, where they act as intermediaries between the main *Gongan* tones 2 and 5. In *slendro pathet manyura*, aside from the principal *Gongan* tones 6 and 2 in cadences 321<u>6</u> and 653<u>2</u>, tone 1 acts as the only *Gongan* tone in *Kutut Manggung*. In *Ladrang Sijem, Gongan* tone 1 acts as an intermediary between main *Gongan* tones 5 and 2. In *pelog pathet lima, Gongan* tones other than 1 and 5 in cadences 5(4)3<u>2</u>1 and 216<u>5</u> respectively are 2, 6 and 3 in *Tlutur Solo* and 6 in *Tjandranata.*

Cadences and a restricted number of ending *Gongan* tones are a musical technique that give a sense of order to these tones, as they are governed by counts of four and bipolarity.

This little analysis of two pieces of music is a preliminary view of the role of counts-of-four, bipolarity and the fifth interval which can be expanded to include as many *gendhing* as possible. Other musical manifestations of their application would characterize gamelan music as a whole. Furthermore, these same elements may be examined as they are found in the Thai *pii-phaad* and the Kampuchean *pin-peat;* for these two traditions share the presence of these elements.

The conference at the California State University, Northridge, for which this paper was written, centered on the comparisons and differences of the European Middle Ages and the Eastern regions. This conference, therefore, presented an opportunity to show how two musical elements—bipolarity and the fifth interval—both used during those times, behaved differently in gamelan, with the added element of counts-of-four.

UNIVERSITY OF THE PHILIPPINES

S L E N D R O			P E L O G		
NEM 6532 216(5)	SANGA 2165 532(1)	MANYURA 3216 653(2)	LIMA 5(4)32(1) 2165	NEM 216(5) 6532	BARANG 3276 653(2)
Avoids 1 NNNG	Avoids 3 NNNG	Avoids 5 NNNG	Avoids 7 NNNG	Avoids 4 NNNG	Avoids 1 & 4 NNNG
101 Ladrang Karawitan 5	201 Renjep 2	301 Kutut Manggung 1	501 Ladrang Manik Maninten 1	601 Sri Kuntjara 6	701 Pangkur 6
6666	2262	1131	1551	6626	6726
5322	2262	1161	1531	6262	2
3335	2222		5111	5266	6722
5225	5562		5111		6326
102 Ladrang Remeng 6	202 Radjaswala 5	302 Ladrang Sijem 2	502 Ladrang Sarilaja 5	602 Ladrang Sri Redjeki 5	702 Ketawang Megatruh 2
6222	6165	2355	2325	5521	22
2333	6165	3231	1562	1535	77
3115	2525	6132	6325	1155	56
5556	2621			5555	72
	6165			5525	
103 Ladrang Agun Agun 2	203 Ketawang Sinom Logondang 5	303 Loro Loro Topeng 6	503A Tlutur Solo 2	603 Ladrang Sarajuda 3	703 Ketawang Langengita 6
2332	1515	216	21	1153	76
2332	55	(3 kenongan)	12	1153	77
2232	25		25		73
2232	52		56		63
	55		55		36
	52		55		76
			53		72
			31		72

704
Ladrang
Kuwang
7
3 7 3 7
3 7 3 3
6 7 3 7

705
Ladrang
Winagun
5
5 7 7 5
5 7 7 7
7 6 6 2
5 7 7 5

706
Ladrang
Wiludjeng
6
6 2 6 6
6 2 6 6
6 2 6 6

604
Ladrang
Susilo
madya
2
2 2 6 5
5 3 3 2

605
Ketawang
Tropongbang
5
2 5
6 5
5 2
5 2
2 5

606
Megamendung
2
6 3 2 2
2 3 6 2
2 1 6 2
2 3 6 2

503B
Ladrang Tlutur
5
5 6 2 5
5 5 2 6
2 5 5 5

504
Tjandranata
5
5 2 2 6
6 6 1 5
5 2 2 6
6 6 1 5

505
Djatikondang
3
3 5 5 3
3 6 5 6
3 5 5 3
3 3 5 3

506
Retnaningsih
5
5 5 2 5
5 5 1 5

304
Sri
Katon
6
6 6 6 2
3 3 6 6

305
Puspawarna
6
1 5
1 3
1 3
1 6
1 6

306
Kanda-Manyura
3
3 1 1 3
3 1 1 3
6 5 1 3
6 6 3 3

204
Gambir
Sawit
5
1 1 3 5
1 1 2 5
1 1 2 5

205
Ladrang
Gondjang
Gandjing
5
5 1 1 1
5 6 5 5
5 1 1 5

206
Ladrang
Uluk-Ulik
5
5 6 1 5
5 6 1 6
6 5 3 2
6 6 1 5
5 6 1 5

104
Ladrang
Eling
Eling
2
2 2 6 6
6 6 2 2

105
Bondet
5
5 6 3 5
5 6 3 5

106
Ladrang
Babad
Kentjent
5
5 5 3 2
2 2 3 5

Fig. 9. Kenong and Gongan Tones of 36 Gending[16]

---

[16] Hood, Paragon, pp. 304–327.

Procession without Progress: The Mastery of Static Style in the Medieval Sequence

by Nancy van Deusen

Western music historical method for decades has concentrated on determining the origins of manuscripts, genres, notational systems and signs, as well as on specific works composed by identifiable composers. The legitimate work of a music historian, accordingly, has been to accumulate information concerning events and composers with the purpose of fashioning a story—a history—with as few gaps as possible. Names, events, and dates, important as they are for their mnemonic qualities, have been the goals of research.

Probably nowhere within the music-historical discipline, which has developed a cluster of germane questions and has tenaciously held to them, have these basic assumptions been so deeply ingrained, yet so utterly inappropriate, as in the study of the medieval sequence. Much, indeed, has been written concerning the sequence, but music historians interested in this particular category of medieval music and texts have concentrated on either the origin of the sequence, or on one or the other of the two persons who have been given credit for writing the majority of the early sequences in one case, and the later sequences in another, namely Notker (ninth–tenth centuries, Sankt Gallen) and Adam of Saint Victor (twelfth century, Paris). The legitimacy and value of these research goals of origin and identity have been largely unquestioned.

In a work and composer-oriented western music-historical tradition, the sequence stands out as an anomaly. It is neither significantly related to a series of identifiable composers, nor adequately described by customary analytical methods. Scholarly work which has concentrated on composers' identities, such as Notker and Adam of Saint Victor, or on the form of the sequence— the so-called double versicle structure distinctive to the sequence—has approached neither the most interesting, nor the most significant features of this highly meaningful genre. In fact, both research orientations have led away from the genre itself, and discouraged interest in the sequence, rather than interpreting its function or describing its essential characteristics. One can ascertain the vitality of this genre by the fact that the sequence was sung throughout the continent of Europe from approximately 900 to 1600, as its broad extant manuscript sources clearly demonstrate.[1]

Hence, this study will concentrate neither on the origin of the sequence nor on attributions of works to particular composers, but will instead look at the

---

[1] See Nancy van Deusen, "The Medieval Latin Sequence: A Complete Catalogue of the Sources and Editions of the Texts and Melodies," *Journal of the Plainsong and Medieval Music Society* 5 (1982), 56–60. There are approximately 3,000 manuscript collections containing 3,000 text-melody combinations, with approximately 1,700 melodies.

sequence itself. Since it would obviously be impossible here to review the three thousand texts and seventeen hundred melodies for the sequence which we find in approximately three thousand sources of this medieval song genre, two examples have been selected, one from the earlier period of sequence composition, that is, around 900 which will be compared with another sequence whose earliest appearance occurs in the late twelfth century. Both are taken from the Germanic rather than the Frankish cultural region.

Sequence style is difficult to describe. It poses a methodological problem for the following reason. Most analytical methods have developed from, and been devised to describe western music, with its hierarchies and telic purposefulness. Furthermore, the most well-defined, highly-cultivated, widely-spread, and deeply-ingrained methods of analysis for western music generally are directed primarily to simultaneously-occurring relationships, in other words, to vertical harmonic sonorities, to their classifications, to descriptions of their interactions with each other, and their transformations. For the sequence, none of these methods are appropriate. First, the sequence remained throughout its long history a predominately monophonic genre, displaying— as this study will at least partially demonstrate—neither hierarchical partitions nor teleological progression. It is a western musical-textual genre whose generic individuality, as we will see, is based primarily on its static style. It therefore presents what, especially, in the later phase of its use, that is, post thirteenth-century, can be considered as an anachronistic value-system.

What are some alternatives to contrapuntal tradition and chordal analysis which are based on classifications according to whether simultaneously-occurring sonorities lead to or away from tonal centers? We find abundant demonstration of alternative organizational principles in the enormous repertory of sequence composition. We will consider the following questions: what is the essence of the melodic style, what are the distinctive structural moments, how can we describe them and what analytical methods can we use to distinguish these structural features? What makes the sequences we are considering compositions? Why do we have the sense that the sequence at hand is a complete composition, with a beginning, a middle processional section, and an end? What *is* a "complete" composition? When we consider text-music relationships, we immediately notice that the one syllable, consistently paired with one tone, makes this style distinctive. What effect does it actually have? What effect does the musical repetition combined with a different text, perhaps even a different word alignment, produce?

Example I, an analysis, sets forth a series of value judgments. What leads one to make these particular decisions? Can one avoid making purely subjective interpretations? First, the validity of the principle that the beginnings and endings of phrases have intrinsic importance has been assumed. These melodic moments have cognitive importance because they remain in one's memory longer, hence have a lasting impact. A consciousness of value, and the attempt to give reasons for decisions regarding value transforms an analytical discussion into an aesthetic consideration. The goal is no longer to identify what is subjectively, personally important, but rather what is musically-textually emphasized, thus moving out of the area of taste to approach the more interesting question of structural validity.

We will consider the earlier example, *Rex regum Deus noster colende*, transcribed from the manuscript Kassel, Landesbibliothek 4°5, a manuscript containing a graduale, ordinarium, and an extensive sequentiarium with fifty-six sequences from central Germany, notated in the second half of the thirteenth century in so-called "Hufnagel" notation on four lines with one clef. Although produced in the late thirteenth century, it is one of the earliest sources from the Germanic cultural region to present this sequence in pitch-decipherable notation, hence the choice of this manuscript as an edition source.[2] Its list of concordances reads like a "Who's Who" of the sources for the early Germanic sequence, including the tenth-century Mainz cathedral source, London, British Library Additional Ms 19768, the Bamberger codices, Ed. III 7, Ed. V 9, the Pruem troper, Paris, Bibliothèque nationale fonds latin 9448, as well as many of the earliest sources from Sankt Emmeram and Sankt Gallen.[3] Versions of the text have been published in the *Analecta Hymnica* collection, as well as by Chevalier, Eggen, Kehrein, de Goede, and von den Steinen;[4] Richard Crocker has edited both music and text.[5] Liturgically, the sequence is for the confessor, commencing: King of Kings, to whom we pray, You moderate the hordes of Christian troops, destined to fight in horrific battle. Von den Steinen's German version seems to come closer in sense and construction to the Latin, as is typical of the relationship between the two languages, German and Latin:

> König der Könige, unser anzubetender Gott!
> Du lenkest die christliche Heerschar,
> indem du die Kriegskundigen zu furchtbarem Kampfe bestimmst,
> und die staatsverständigen Ratsherrn deinen Völkern zu Lehrmeistern gibst.

Even a cursory look at the sequence indicates the several important textual and musical features. First, the limited tonal vocabulary is obvious. There is an

---

[2] A complete critical edition of the sequence is in preparation.

[3] See van Deusen, "The Medieval Latin Sequence." A complete catalogue of the contents of all of the extant sources of sequences, as well as a incipit catalogue including all of the concordances of each text-music combination is forthcoming, to be published in the series *Répertoire international des sources musicales* (*RISM*).

[4] *Analecta hymnica medii aevi*, ed. G. M. Dreves, Clemens Blume, H. M. Bannister, 55 vols (Leipzig, 1886–1922), 53:390; U. Chevalier, *Repertorium hymnologicum*, 6 vols (Louvain, 1892), 17499; Erik Eggen, *The Sequences of the Archbishopric of Nidarós*, 2 vols (Copenhagen, 1968), 201; N. de Goede, *The Utrecht Prosarium. Cod. Utraiect. Univ. Bibl. 417* (*Monumenta musica Neerlandica*. Amsterdam, 1965), 123; J. Kehrein, *Lateinische Sequenzen des Mittelalters* (Mainz, 1873), 326; Wolfram von den Steinen, *Notker der Dichter und seine geistige Welt,* 2 vols. (Bern, 1948, repr. 1978), Editionsband 88.

[5] See Richard L. Crocker, *The Early Medieval Sequence* (Berkeley, 1977), especially pp. 268f. Crocker's edition differs from the one included here due, no doubt, to the fact that he consulted no diastematic sources of the sequence.

interesting emphasis on pentatonic aspects of the entire ambitus of the extended octave c–d', that is c-d-f-g-a, in which half-steps appear to be avoided. A majority of the lines end on d. Many also begin on d, contributing to a sense of the melodic style's unification. Most importantly, there seem to be no overt characteristic textual or melodic features which would draw the attention either to textual devices or musical significance. The two parameters, text and melody, seem to be equally devoid of either poetic characteristics, such as rhyme, assonance, or patterned repetition, and the same seems to be true of the melody. The most distinctive feature of melodic-textual congruence is the energizing rhythmic stress produced by both syllable and tone in the alternation of 3-2-4-syllable words, such as in the lines:

Dando magistros tuis populis	2 3 2 3
Ex quibus est sacer iste sacerdos	1 2 1 2 2 3
Qui in pace degens ecclesie sancte	1 1 2 2 4 2
or	
Iste hereticis invisus atque paganis nec non	
regi omnium pravorum	2 4 3 2 3 1 1 2 3 3

Accent is changed by word-groups. A close bond of syllable-tone produces rhythm, without apparent schemes of accentual patterns. Rhythm, or the forward motion of textual-musical syntax is produced textually, not strictly musically. Furthermore, when one compares a melodic line with its repetition, one notices that the melodic line is changed by the text, as word-groupings constantly shift:

Consules scios rei publice / Dando magistros tuis populis.

This unique pairing of tone with syllable without exploitation of the characteristic properties of either is made even more obvious when we compare what we have observed with another, later sequence. Notice how both textual and musical parameters are exploited in this case.

Let us consider the sequence, *Promissa mundo gaudia*, a sequence for Nativity and Circumcision. There are three melodies for the text, which also has been edited several times.[6] The earliest instance of the sequence dates from the twelfth century; its appearance, especially in German and Bohemian sources, is plentiful and continuous, and it was copied into sources well into the sixteenth century, where it also occurs in published missals. Because of its readability and comprehensive collection of sequences, the so-called "Franus Cantionale" from Hradec Králové (or Königgrätz), copied around 1505, has been chosen for this edition. The manuscript contains an ordinarium, graduale, a magnificent sequentiarium with ninety-three sequences, and a

---

    6 AH 54:143; Chevalier 15617; Kehrein 30; F. J. Mone, *Lateinische Hymnen des Mittelalters*, 3 vols, II, 65; G. Zwick, *Les proses en usage à l'église de St. Nicolas à Fribourg* (Immensee, 1950), 17.

cantionale. Monophonic pieces, the major part of the manuscript, are notated in Bohemian notation, with typical rhomboid *puncta*, on four lines. There are, as well, polyphonic pieces notated in mensural notation. The manuscript also contains miniatures, as well as decorative initials. It is a spectacular codex.

This particular sequence has been selected for the following reason. Although the sequence is approximately the same length as *Rex regum*, its style contrasts significantly, both textually and musically, with the example above. First, musical repetitions occur in the incipit at *gaudia* and *gracia,* as well as textual pattern. Each line ends with *die ista.* There are multiple instances of a perceptible antecedent-consequent relationship between pairs of lines, as, for example between l/2 and 3/4, a relationship which is reinforced by the entrance of line 3 at the fifth. *g-d'* or *g-b-d'* are frequent intervallic statements and tend to unify the sequence, as, for example, in the structures of lines 5/6 and 7/8, and especially 9/l0. There are short melodic sequences such as lines 5/6 *Lapis ille / iunctus parietibus.* Musical pattern, repetition, and overt devices of many kinds are mirrored in textual devices, most obviously in the rhyme or assonance of each half-line: *gaudia/gracia, fecunditas/deitas, sine matre/sine patre, dedit/infudit, defunctum/baculum, contritus est/abscisus est,* etc. Finally, instead of rhythm generated by a fast exchange especially between two- and three-syllable words, *Promissa mundo gaudia* exhibits regularity or extended rhythmic pattern, as *Promissa mundo gaudia/superna solvit gracia.* The close bond between tone and syllable, overcome by neither recognizable musical nor textual pattern is not conspicuous in the later example. Pattern and device, both textual and musical, have, in a sense, fragmented the perfect unity of text/syllable in the earlier example. Our attention and interest are drawn away from the text-tone union itself. They are engaged by distinctive and overt textual and musical devices. This produces a song-like character, but also a movement away from a liturgical category into a genre in which textual and musical considerations predominate. The sequence is, in some respects, by the twelfth century, well on its way to become a shaped, constructed work of art. There is a sense, too, that it is art for its own sake, or, at least, comparatively speaking, much more of an autonomous composition.

In other respects, however, this is not at all the case. The most convincing differences between early and later sequences occur most frequently in their incipits, not in the rest of the composition. In some respects the same stylistic features which the sequence evidenced at the beginning of its long history were apparent at the end of its development. These include a musical extensory process which was not developmental, but rather, additive, in which musical style exhibits increasing tension, as well as an increase in activity— usually in predictable positions of the composition—without a resolution of this activity. There is, apparently, no teleologically-defined purpose, no distinctive musical goal. Through this alternative musical processionality, a connection to other world musical cultures may be established, but the relationship is of spirit and tendency, rather than expressed by means of musical quotation. The sequence is a curiosity. Why did it remain in many ways stylistically unchanged throughout its long history? A well-defined ceremonial purpose gave it rationality which is reflected in musical, textual style.

"Progress," of course, is not easy to define. Returning to the analysis of structural features made for the older sequence, *Rex regum Deus noster colende*, one observes the frequency with which beginnings of phrases use the same notes, namely, either *c, g, a,* and how often entire phrases return to *d*. The reiteration of this *d* at cadential points contributes significantly to the stationary impression given by the piece. Also, despite the ubiquitous *d*, analysis within one particular mode is not especially appropriate, nor of much value. Although the sequence returns to *d* and pivots between *a* and *d*, it does not really exhibit the basic qualities of the *d*-dorian mode, but rather *cd fg fg*. The reiteration of *ega* also tends to obscure a strong modal impression. The half-step relationship, *ef* occurs only fleetingly. There appears to be a deliberate avoidance of either *b* or *b*-flat relationship. It is interesting that the pentatonic relationship *c-d-f-g-a* is emphasized.

These remarks are true, not only of this particular sequence, but of the entire spectrum of sequences. Further, in the case of the later sequence, even though the incipit may appear to be "tonal," evidencing what appears to be an antecedent-consequent phrase construction, the more "tonal" melodic aspect ends with the incipit. Static style is achieved by a consistent pendulum-swing between the bottom and top edges of the most-used *ambitus,* by repeated beginnings and endings of phrases, and by an additive rather than developmentary music-extensory process. Furthermore, the sequence, both musically and textually, exhibits a construction of interchangeable parts. The double lines, both textually and musically can be placed in any order without disturbance to a sense of the entire composition. While the sequence has a definite beginning and an end, the entire middle processional phase can be negotiated. Each pair of lines has autonomy, stands, to a certain extent alone as a module, or, to use medieval terminology, a *cento*, translated to the Latin *punctum*.[7]

The static style, a certain non-progressiveness of the sequence as a genre can be observed throughout its long history. This points out a general principle, namely, that liturgical genres were significant, informing the musical-textual pieces within them. The sequence is an example of this. Precisely the feature that gave sequences generic identity—their transitional function between the alleluia and gospel of the mass—informed, as well, their musical-textual style. The sequence was a transitional liturgical genre. They "marked time" so to speak, at the mid-point of the mass, between the alleluia and the evangelium. The sequence's transitional bridge-like status is reflected

---

[7] Cf. the definition and explanation of *cento/centones*, consistently translated *punctum*, as a compositional principle in Isidore of Seville, *Etymologiarum sive Originum libri XX*, ed. W. M. Lindsay (Oxford, 1911, repr. 1966), I:39 (38), a definition, referring to Valeria Faltonia Proba, *Centonum poetria* (*Patrologiae cursus completus, Series latina* XIX, cols. 802–816) which was widely quoted throughout the Middle Ages.

textually, as well as musically, in a style noticeable for its process without progress.

Not only was the sequence the bridge of the mass, reflecting transition in as many ways as possible, an aspect explained in detail elsewhere,[8] but, perhaps the sequence in western music is a bridge to other world musical traditions which are not characterized by unique beginnings, resounding cadences, and a step-by-step process within the composition, leading, finally, to a goal. We have, in the sequence, an alternative means of musical construction. We can observe a musical extensory process which exists in, and makes use of the present moment without leading inexorably to a musical future. It is a feature found, for example, as well, in Indonesian music.[9]

The sequence, as is well known, was excised, for the most part, from the mass ceremony. I have often wondered, in working for some years with this particular genre, whether this was due not so much to counter-reformatory zeal, but rather that the sequence's sensitive position, based on a clearly-perceived function within the mass, with a static style exemplifying this function by its stationary quality, were both—by the closing years of the sixteenth century—obsolete. At any rate, the sequence offers us a window not only to a medieval realization that ceremonial events must, in all particulars, be meaningful, but a medieval connection, as well, to the music of the rest of the world.

THE CLAREMONT GRADUATE SCHOOL

---

[8] See van Deusen, "The Use and Significance of the Sequence," *Musica Disciplina* 40 (1986), 1–46.

[9] José Maceda's contribution to this volume brings an important dimension to this consideration.

* as many as three

Fig. 1. Structural Analysis: *Rex regum*

1. Rex re - gum De - us no - ster co - len - de,
2. Tu mo - de - ra - ris mi - li - ci - am Chri - sti - a - nam,
3. Bel - lan - di gna - ros hor - ri - bi - li proe - li - o de - sti - nan - do
4. Con - su - les sci - os re - i pu - bli - ce
5. Dan - do ma - gis - tros tu - is po - pu - lis.
6. Nec e - nim fal - le - ris e - li - gen - di sa - pi - ens,
7. Quem cu - i sub - ro - ges mi - ni - ste - ri - o, De - us.
8. Ex qui - bus est sa - cer i - ste sa - cer - dos,
9. Qui in pa - ce de - gens ec - cle - si - e san - cte
10. Con - si - li - a - tus est qua - li - ter ho - stis ir - rup - ci - o - nem,
11. Que so - let in - cau - tos de - po - pu - la - ri pre - mu - ni - vis - set.
12. I - ste he - re - ti - cis in - vi - sus at - que pa - ga - nis nec - non

Fig. 2. *Rex regum Deus noster*

1. Pro - mis - sa mun - di gau - di - a su - per - na sol - vit gra - ci - a di - e i - sta.

2. In vir - gi - ne fe - cun - di - tas in pi - e ful - sit de - i - tas di - e i - sta.
AH: prole

3. In su - per - nis e - di - tur si - ne ma - tre hac in val - le na - tus est si - ne
AH: genitus
pa - tre di - e i - sta.

4. Vir - ga Ies - se flo - ri - da fru - ctum de - dit, Ge - de - o - nis vel - le - ra ros
in - fu - dit di - e i - sta.

5. La - pis il - le re - pro - bus iun - ctus pa - ri - e - ti - bus u - nus fe - cit
:m
an - gu - lum di - e i - sta.

6. He - li - se - us es - i - it et de - fun - ctum ad - i - it sub - se - cu - tus
ba - cu - lum di - e i - sta

7. Pres - sus pe - de mu - li - e - ris co - lu - ber con - tri - tus est di - e i - sta.

Fig. 3. *Promissa mundo gaudia*

King Arthur and the "Sarmatian Connection": An Overview and Update

by C. Scott Littleton

Since 1978, in a series of articles published in the *Journal of American Folklore* and elsewhere,[1] I have attempted to demonstrate that the medieval legends of King Arthur, the Knights of the Round Table, and the quest for the Holy Grail derive from an oral epic tradition shared by the ancient Sarmatians, Alans, and other north Iranian-speaking pastoral nomads who roamed the southern Russian steppes in the centuries immediately preceding the Christian Era.

This hypothesis, which challenges the conventional scholarly wisdom that the legends in question are rooted in Celtic mythology,[2] was stimulated by two important discoveries: 1) the presence of a great many "Arthurian" themes and motifs in the Nart sagas of the Ossets (or Ossetians), a contemporary people whose Alan ancestors settled in the northern foothills of the Caucasus Mountains almost fifteen hundred year ago,[3] and 2) the presence in A.D. 175 in Northern Britain of a troop of Sarmatian *cataphracti*, or heavy auxiliary

---

Acknowledgements: I would like to thank James F. Mallory, Ann C. Thomas, Helmut Nickel, Udo Strutynski, Jaan Puhvel, Gunar Freibergs, Felix J. Oinas, the late Georges Dumézil, and, last but far from least, Linda Malcor (née Peterson), with whom I have written the book mentioned below, for their valuable comments and suggestions at various points in the evolution of this project, to say nothing of their support and encouragement. Indeed, without that support and encouragement, it is doubtful whether the "Sarmatian connection" could ever have been made in the first place, let alone sustained.

The ideas expressed in this article are more fully developed in *From Scythia to Camelot: A Radical Reassessment of the Legends of King Arthur, the Knights of the Round Table, and the Holy Grail* by C. Scott Littleton and Linda A. Malcor (New York, 1994).

[1] C. Scott Littleton and Ann C. Thomas, "The Sarmatian Connection: New Light on the Origin of the Arthurian and Holy Grail Legends," *Journal of American Folklore* 91 (1978), 513–527; C. Scott Littleton, "The Holy Grail, the Cauldron of Annwn, and the Nartyamonga: A Further Note on the Sarmatian Connection," *Journal of American Folklore* 92 (1979), 326–333; "From Swords in the Earth to the Sword in the Stone: A Possible Reflection of an Alano-Sarmatian Rite of Passage in the Arthurian Tradition," in *Homage to Georges Dumézil*, Edgar Polomé, ed., Journal of Indo-European Studies Monograph 3 (Washington, D. C., 1982), 53–67.

[2] E.g., A. L. Rowse's assertion that the story of King Arthur is ". . . the chief and lasting contribution of the Celts to the mind and literature of Europe" (quoted by Elizabeth Jenkins, *The Mystery of King Arthur* [New York, 1975], p. 214).

[3] Georges Dumézil, *Légendes sur les Nartes* (Paris, 1930), pp. 8–11; Tadeusz Sulimirski, *The Sarmatians* (New York, 1970), pp. 175–178. For translations of the Nart sagas, see Dumézil, *Légendes; Le Livres des héros* (Paris, 1965); *Romans de Scythie et d'Alentour* (Paris, 1978); Adolf Dirr, *Caucasian Folk Tales* (New York, 1925).

cavalry, whose descendants managed to survive as a separate ethnic enclave until the end of the Roman period.[4]

More recently, my colleague Linda A. Malcor (see below) has convincingly demonstrated that the Alanic settlements in Armorica, the Lot region, and elsewhere in Gaul in the fifth century A.D. provided a second channel for important elements of this same steppe tradition to spread to Western Europe;[5] these elements surfaced primarily in the Continental legends and romances surrounding Lancelot—i.e., "the Alan of Lot"—and the Grail.[6]

The purpose of this paper is to review the several dimensions of what has come to be called, from the title of my initial essay, "the Sarmatian connection,"[7] and to provide an update on some new and important interpretations that reinforce this hypothesis, including the possibility that several "Arthurian" themes can be detected in Japanese mythology.[8] However, let us begin by looking at some of the more important similarities among the Nart sagas and the Arthurian legends and how these similarities can be explained.

THE NARTS AND THE KNIGHTS

The first scholar to recognize the similarities between the Ossetic and Arthurian traditions was the eminent French medievalist Joël Grisward, currently a professor at the University of Tours. A former student of the greatest modern expert on Ossetic folklore, the late Georges Dumézil, Grisward pointed out what he called "the motif of the sword thrown in the lake."[9] Mortally wounded, Batraz, the chief Nart hero, whose name probably derives from the same northern Iranian source as that of the ancient Scythian

---

[4] I. A. Richmond, "The Sarmatae, *Bremmetennacum veteranorum*, and the *Regio bremetennacensis*," *Journal of Roman Studies* 35 (1945), 16–29; Sulimirski, *The Sarmatians*, pp. 177–78. See also Helmut Nickel, "Wer waren König Artus' Ritter? Über die geschichtliche Grundlage der Artussagen," *Zeitschrift der historischen Waffen- und Kostümkunde* 1 (1975), 1–18.

[5] For a discussion of the Alanic settlements in Gaul, see Bernard S. Bachrach, *A History of the Alans in the West* (Minneapolis, 1973); "The Alans in Gaul," *Traditio* 22 (1967), 476–489; "Another Look at the Barbarian Settlements in Southern Gaul," *Traditio* 25 (1970), 354–358.

[6] Linda A. Peterson, "The Alan of Lot: A New Interpretation of the Legends of Lancelot," *Folklore and Mythology Studies* 9 (1985), 31–49; "The Alans and the Grail, or the Theft, the Swindle, and the Legend," *Folklore and Mythology Studies* 10 (1986), 27–42.

[7] See, for example, Geoffrey Ashe, *The Discovery of King Arthur* (London, 1986), 158–159. In light of what we know, perhaps it ought to be labeled the "Alano-Sarmatian" or "North Iranian Connection."

[8] Littleton, "Some possible Arthurian Themes in Japanese Mythology and Folklore," *Journal of Folklore Research* 20 (1983), 67–82.

[9] Joël Grisward, "Le motif de l'épée jetée au lac: la mort d'Arthur et la mort de Batraz," *Romania* 90 (1969), 289–340. See also his "Trois perspectives médiévales," *Nouvelle école*, Nos. 21–22 (Paris, 1973), 80–89.

water god Don Bettyr,[10] is carried by his faithful Nart companions to the shore of a lake. He commands them to throw his magical sword into the sea so that he may be released from his suffering. However, the grieving Narts are loath to obey this final order, and they attempt to deceive their dying chief by hiding the wondrous weapon and reporting back that his last wish has been fulfilled. But when Batraz asks what occurred when the sword entered the water, their answer reveals their deception, for only Batraz knows what will happen. Finally, and with great reluctance and effort (the weapon is so heavy that only Batraz can wield it with ease), the Narts carry out his command, and when at last the sword is hurled into the water the lake turns blood red and becomes extremely turbulent. After he learns of this prodigious event, Batraz ascends to Heaven, secure in the knowledge that his destiny has been fulfilled.[11]

One need not be a specialist in the Arthurian romances to see some striking parallels between this account and the famous death scene in Malory's *La mort d'Arthur,* where Sir Bedivere hides Excalibur twice before finally returning it to the lake.[12] The prodigious event is different—a hand rises from the water and grasps Arthur's sword—but the structure of these two accounts, so widely separated in time and space, is nearly identical. And it is far from the only parallel between the two traditions. For example, Arthur's staunchest paladins, Sir Kay and the aforementioned Sir Bedivere, are strikingly similar to the Ossetic pair Urysmæg and Sosryko (or Soslan).[13] The names Kay and Bedivere are not Celtic, and both can be derived from traditions immediately associated with the Alano-Sarmatian community. The name Kay seems to be a variant of the ancient Iranian warrior name Kai, (e.g., the legendary warrior-king Kai Chosrau), which could easily have been preserved by the Iranian-speaking Alans and Sarmatians. Bedivere (or Bedwyr) most likely derives from the Turkish—indeed, pan-Altaic—word *bahadur,* or "military commander," reflexes of which can be found in a number of Eastern European languages, e.g., Russian *bogatyr,* Hungarian *batur.*[14] Given the location of the ancient North Iranians, and, indeed, the fact that their westward expansion was in fair measure precipitated by that of the Turkish-speaking Huns, it is reasonable to assume that they might have borrowed this Turkish word, in much the same way the Allies in World War II borrowed such German military expressions as "to strafe" (from *strafen,* "to punish") and *blitzkrieg* ("lightning warfare").

---

[10] That is, the personification of the Don River. See Dumézil, *Romans de Scythie et d'Alentour,* pp. 214–215.

[11] Dumézil, *Légendes,* p. 69.

[12] The most famous version of this tale, of course, is Sir Thomas Malory, *La morte d'Arthur,* ed. Janet Cowen (Harmondsworth, 1969), p. 516.

[13] For discussions of Uryzmæg and Sosryko, see Dumézil, *Romans de Scythie et d'Alentour,* pp. 93–106, 262–264.

[14] For a discussion of these etymologies, see Littleton and Thomas, "The Sarmatian Connection," p. 518, and Nickel "Artus' Ritter," p. 11.

Arthur's father, Uther Pendragon, bears a name that links him with a variety of Eastern European warrior traditions. Nickel suggests that Geoffrey of Monmouth's interpretation of "Pendragon" as a bastardized construction from Welsh *pen,* or "head," plus Latin *draco,* "dragon," is an incorrect folk etymology. The first element is more likely derived from *pan* (or *panje*), which sometimes appears as *pen* and means "leader," a word that turns up in a variety of Eastern European dialects, and which can be found in the names of several historically attested Alan chiefs (e.g., Respendial). Coupled with *draco* (i.e., "Pandraco"), this would yield a form meaning "Dragon Leader"—a name consonant with several Roman images of Sarmatian warriors bearing banners emblazoned with elongated dragons (e.g., the well-known image on Trajan's Column in Rome).[15]

In a number of contexts, the word in question, which Vernadsky thinks derives ultimately from Old Turkish *bon,* or "strong," retains the initial consonant (e.g., the fifth century Alan chief Sangiban, whose name also includes what is probably a reflex of the Old Turkish form for "ten thousand," *san).*[16] As Malcor points out, the word in question is also reflected in the name of Lancelot's father, King Ban.[17] Like *bahadur, Pan/ban* seems to have been borrowed from the Huns.

There is no etymological connection between the name of Batraz's father, Hamyc, and Uther Pendragon, although both sired their respective offspring with the aid of magic: Batraz was born from a hump on Hamyc's back,[18] while Arthur was conceived only after Merlin caused Ygerna to believe Uther was her husband.

Arthur's kinswoman, The Lady of the Lake, from whom he receives Excalibur, closely resembles Batraz's aunt Satana, "the Wise Woman of the Narts," who helps him to obtain his magical sword.[19] Moreover, the famous "sword-in-the-stone" episode, in which the young Arthur proves his right to the kingship,[20] is consonant with Ammianus Marcellinus's account of how the ancient Alans were wont to ". . . plunge a naked sword into the earth with barbaric ceremonies [and] worship that with great respect, as Mars, the presiding deity of the regions over which they wander" (31.4.21).[21] Some years ago I suggested the pulling out of such an embedded sword, which clearly survives in the Arthurian legend, may have been a rite of passage

---

[15] Nickel, "Artus' Ritter," pp. 10–11; Littleton and Thomas, "The Sarmatian Connection," pp. 517–518.

[16] George Vernadsky, "The Eurasian Nomads and Their Impact on Medieval Europe," *Studi medievali* 4 (1963), 401–434.

[17] Peterson, "The Alan of Lot," 36–37.

[18] Dumézil, *Légendes,* pp. 50–51.

[19] Dumézil, *Légendes,* pp. 61–65.

[20] For an extended discussion of this episode from the standpoints of the "Sarmatian Connection," see Littleton, "From Swords in the Earth," pp. 55–58.

[21] See D. Yonge, trans., *The Roman History of Ammianus Marcellinus* (London, 1902), p. 582.

wherein a young Alan warrior demonstrated his right to be chief of the war band.[22]

It is also curious that both the Ossetic and the Arthurian traditions include a magical cup (or cauldron), known respectively as the Nartyamonga ("Cup of the Narts") and the Holy Grail, which magically appears at feasts to the bravest and/or purest members of the respective war-bands. The brother of the wounded Grail-King is called Mangon (or Amangon), and, in one of the immediate precursors to the fully-developed Grail romances of the twelfth and thirteenth centuries, the tenth-century Welsh poem entitled "The Spoils of Annwn" there is a magical cauldron that almost exactly matches the Ossetic descriptions of the Nartyamonga.[23]

The foregoing should give at least some indication of the kinds of thematic—and, indeed, onomastic—connections that have been adduced between the Ossetic sagas and the ritual practices of their ancient Alanic forebearers on the one hand, and the medieval Arthurian and Grail traditions on the other. The next matter that needs to be considered is how this steppe-spawned tradition managed to impact medieval Europe?

BREMETENNACUM VETERANORUM

When Grisward first discovered the parallels between the traditions in question, he attempted to explain them as the result of some very ancient, albeit unattested Celtic-Iranian contacts.[24] However, thanks to the third century A.D. Roman historian Dio Cassius, we are now able to pinpoint the onset of this contact with some accuracy.

According to Dio Cassius (who wrote about fifty years after the fact), we have the following historical information: At the conclusion of the Marcomannian War in A.D. 175, Marcus Aurelius conscripted 8,000 *cataphracti*, or heavy auxiliary cavalrymen, from among the recently defeated Jazyges; the Jazyges were a Sarmatian tribe that had joined forces with the Quadi and the Marcomanni in an attempt to invade Pannonia (modern Hungary).[25] Of these conscripts, 5,500 were posted to northern Britain to man the forts along Hadrian's Wall.[26] When their period of service was finished, the Jazyges did not return to their homeland in the steppes, but were settled in a *vicus*, or veterans' settlement. This settlement was located at Bremetennacum veteranorum, a major cavalry post on the Rible River near the modern

---

[22] Littleton, "From Swords in the Earth," pp. 58–60.

[23] For a discussion of these matters, see Littleton, "The Holy Grail, the Cauldron of Annwn, and the Nartyamonga."

[24] Grisward, "Trois perspectives médiévales," pp. 88–89.

[25] See Herbert Baldwin Foster, trans., *Dio's Rome* (Troy, N. Y., 1905), 2:240–241. See also Sulimirski, *The Sarmatians,* pp. 177–178, who points out that the Jazyges had migrated into the region about a century earlier. Their ancestral home was in the steppes east of the Dniepper.

[26] Ibid.

Lancashire village of Ribchester in an area immediately adjacent to the site of the Roman camp archaeological excavations. From this *vicus*, we have a considerable amount of evidence in the form of grave *stelae*, weapons, armor, and a variety of inscriptions indicating that a Sarmatian community existed there for several centuries.[27]

On the basis of this evidence, I suggest that the historical Arthur, the victor of Badon Hill and/or the shadowy fifth century British "king" who, as Geoffrey Ashe has recently demonstrated, is called Riothamus in several Continental texts, was a particularly charismatic leader of the Bremetennacum *vicus* in the period immediately following the withdrawal of Roman authority in A.D. 410.[28] In its original British form, the name would be Rigotamos, or "Supreme King," which is clearly honorific.[29] That is, he could easily have been known as "Artorius-Riothamus," the former element being the title proper; similarly, Genghis Khan, whose given name was Temujin, is more widely known by an honorific title that means "Very Mighty Ruler."[30]

Indeed, the name "Arthur" itself, which has always posed problems from the standpoint of Celtic mythology,[31] is in all probability a Celticized variant of the Latin name "Artorius," which in turn can be derived from the gentilic name of the Jazyges' first Roman commander, Lucius Artorius Castus. A career officer and a member of Marcus Aurelius's staff, Artorius was given command of the VI Legion Victrix at Eboracum (York) in A.D. 175, and thus became, in effect, the military governor of northern Britain.[32] Although we cannot yet document it, I am convinced that he led the Jazyges auxiliaries to Britain, and that by the time they reached Eboracum and were posted to the Wall, they had essentially become his private "Praetorius Guard," or at least recognized as an elite corps within the Roman colonial military establishment. The fact that Artorius led a military expedition to Armorica in 184 reinforces Malone's interpretation, as Riothamus made a similar expedition to Gaul in

---

[27] For a detailed discussion of the findings at Ribchester, see Richmond, "The Sarmatae," pp. 18–25.

[28] Ashe, "A Certain very ancient Book," *Speculum* 56 (1981), 301–323; *The Discovery of King Arthur,* pp. 96–106.

[29] Ashe, *The Discovery of King Arthur,* p. 97.

[30] Geoffrey Ashe, "Arthur-Riomathus," *Avalon to Camelot* 1 (1983), 20–23.

[31] While some Arthurian scholars have attempted to derive the name "Arthur" from Irish *art,* "stone" (see, for example, E. K. Chambers, *Arthur of Britain: The Story of King Arthur in History and Legend* [London, 1966], pp. 210 f.), or, citing Nennius' gloss *ursus horribilis,* from Celtic *artos,* "bear," (e.g., John Arnott Macculoch, "Celtic Mythology," in *Mythology of All Races* 3 [Boston, 1918], pp. 186–187), most contemporary scholars see the name as intrinsically Latin (e.g., *The Oxford Dictionary of English Christian Names* [Oxford, 1950], p. 31) or simply "foreign" (e.g., Leslie Alcock, *Arthur's Britain: History and Archeology, A.D. 367–634* [London, 1971], p. 358).

[32] On Lucius Artorius Castus, see Kemp Malone, "Artorius," *Modern Philology* 22 (1924), 367–377, who seems to have been the first to make the connection between the name of this relatively obscure Roman general and that of "the Once and Future King." See also Nickel, "Artus' Ritter," pp. 9–11.

the mid-fifth century, and the two feats of arms may later have conflated, especially if the latter leader was in fact known as Artorius Riothamus.[33]

In any case, the practice of taking a personal name as a title was already well established in Roman politics—e.g., the title "Caesar." Also, the Sarmatian veterans' ethnic cohesion (if not language) was perpetuated by the niche they and their descendants came to occupy in the Roman colonial administration. (Like the Cossacks and the Gurkhas in more modern colonial regimes, each generation probably provided its quota of fighting men.) The Sarmatian veterans seem to have adopted a mini-version of this practice vis-à-vis the memory of their adored first commander.

THE ALANS COME WEST

Meanwhile, about the time the inhabitants of *vicus* at Bremetennacum were beginning to cope with the withdrawal of the legions they had so faithfully served for almost three centuries, their cousins, the Alans, began to appear in Western Europe. Allied with the Visigoths and other Germanic peoples, they were settled by the Roman enclaves in Gaul, Spain, and northern Italy by the middle of the fifth century. In Gaul, there were heavy concentrations of Alans in Armorica (eastern Brittany) and in various parts of what eventually became known as Languedoc. As Malcor points out elsewhere (see below), this settlement pattern is abundantly attested by place names such as Alençon, Alaincourt, and Alanville.[34]

Thus, by the end of the Roman period in the late fifth century A.D., northern Iranian enclaves can be attested from northern Britain to southern Gaul, and their impact on the folklore and legends of their neighbor, especially during this time of troubles, seems to have been profound. The seeds of what eventually grew into the Arthurian and Grail romances had been planted.

SYNCRETISM AND THE ORIGINS OF CHIVALRY

To be sure, a great many Celtic themes and figures managed to penetrate the evolving tradition, both in Britain and on the Continent; among them can be found Gawain and Guinevere (but not, as Malcor points out (see below), her paramour Lancelot). Moreover, the idea of the "Isles of the Blessed," which manifests itself in the conception of Avalon as Arthur's final resting place, is rooted in a decidely Celtic notion of the afterworld,[35] and the image of Merlin was almost certainly shaped, at least in part, by the memory of the

---

[33] Ashe, *The Discovery of King Arthur*, p. 116.

[34] For a list of Alanic toponyms in Western Europe, see Bachrach, *A History of the Alans in the West*, pp. 137–140.

[35] See, for example, Ashe, *The Discovery of King Arthur*, pp. 152–154.

Druids.[36] In short, the end product of the interface among the heroic traditions shared by the Sarmatians and Alans on the one hand, and the indigenous Britons, Romans, and Gauls on the other, was certainly a grand syncretism.

Nevertheless, the core of the Arthurian tradition almost certainly reflects the presence of these northern Iranians who, in addition to their impact on European legendry, were responsible for introducing what eventually became the standard form of medieval mounted combat. Unlike the Mongols and other Central Asian nomads who relied primarily on their bows, the northern Iranians wore heavy scale armor and carried long slashing swords and lances, as well as shields emblazoned with *tamgas*, or tribal heraldic devices (as I have indicated, the principal Sarmatian emblem seems to have been a flying dragon). Indeed, the well-known image of the mounted knight, sheathed in armor from head to toe, his torso covered by a heraldic "coat-of-arms," his lance at the ready, and his broadsword dangling almost to his ankles (which is universally associated with the fully developed Arthurian romances of the fourteenth and fifteenth centuries), was long anticipated by the images of mounted warriors on grave *stelae* found at Ribchester and other sites associated with the Jazyges.[37]

Moreover, wherever we find them, from Britain to Brittany, from Lancashire to Languedoc, these enclaves of Alans and Sarmatians seem to have rapidly become an integral part of the post-Roman European elite.[38] This, of course, magnified the impact of their folklore on the emerging medieval traditions.

By the time the famous twelfth- and thirteenth-century Arthurian and Holy Grail texts were produced, the Alano-Sarmatian heroic *epos* had long since been stripped of whatever "foreign" associations it may have once had. The conflation with indigenous European themes and motifs was well-nigh complete, and the veneer of Christian piety that surrounds the tradition had been added.

THE "JAPANESE CONNECTION"

A brief return to the "Japanese connection" mentioned at the outset of the paper now seems prudent. The chief Japanese "Arthurian" hero is Yamato-takeru, or the "Strong Man of Yamato," the younger of twin sons fathered by the legendary Emperor Keiko. After receiving a magical sword from his aunt, the High Priestess of the cult of the Sun Goddess Amaterasu at Ise, Yamato-takeru leads a band of famous warriors in an expedition against the Yemeshi, or "Eastern Barbarians" (probably the Ainu). He dies by the

---

[36] For a more detailed discussion of Merlin from this perspective, see Littleton, "From Swords in the Earth," pp. 63–64.

[37] See Nickel, "The Dawn of Chivalry," *The Metropolitan Museum of Art Bulletin* 32 (1975), 150–152.

[38] See Bachrach, *A History of the Alans in the West*, pp. 116–117.

seashore shortly after losing the sword, and his body flies magically back to Yamato, where it disappears.[39]

Admittedly, the parallels here are general. However, like Arthur and Batraz, the Japanese hero receives his sword from (or with the help of) a kinswoman who is closely associated with the supernatural, and there is a clear implication that the weapon in question—the most wondrous and Excalibur-like of all Japanese legendary swords—must be "returned" before he can die.[40] Moreover, in two of the three cases (the Ossetic and the Japanese) the sword-bestower is an aunt.[41]

How and when these themes diffused to Japan remains unclear, although I suspect that they were carried eastward by one or more groups of Alans who followed the Silk Road to the northern periphery of China and then on to Korea and Japan in the middle of the fourth century A.D.[42] We do know that at the end of the first millenium B.C., the easternmost of the Atlantic tribes paid tribute to the Han Emperors, who called them the Wo-sun (=Oss, i.e., "Ossetian"),[43] and thus were poised on the western threshold of East Asia.

It appears that the core themes expressed in the legends of King Arthur and the Knights of the Round Table are not only non-European in origin, but also far more widespread than heretofore suspected. Indeed, if my interpretation of the Yamato-takeru legend is correct, they span the Eurasian land mass from end to end.

OCCIDENTAL COLLEGE

---

[39] The ancient sources here are *Kojiki* 2.49 and *Nihonshoki* 3.10–11. See also Littleton, "Some Possible Arthurian Themes," pp. 73–75.

[40] I.e., the sacred Kusanagi sword, a replica of which is presented to every Japanese Emperor at the time he ascends the throne. Atsuhiko Yosjida (*Yamato-takeru to Okuninushi: Hikaku Shinwagaku no kokoromi* [Tokyo, 1979], p. 125) compares Yamato-takeru's relationship to Kusanagi with that of Arthur to Excalibur.

[41] Another curious link between the Japanese and Ossetic traditions is the theme of the "metalled man." As a young man, Batraz demands that the divine smith Kurdalagon encase him in steel, thereby rendering every part of his body invulnerable except for his eyes (see Dumézil, *Légendes,* pp. 61–63). Although Yamato-takeru himself does not share this trait, an analogous figure, called Tetsujin, that is, "Iron Man," is widespread in Japanese folklore (see Taryo Obayashi, "Honcho Tetsujin Denki," *Kikan Minwa* [1975], pp. 95–106). Like Batraz, who massacres a great many of his fellow Narts, and whose death is decreed by God himself (Dumézil, *Légendes,* p. 54), Tetsujin is an ambivalent figure who is killed after an opponent learns the location of his vulnerable spot. Why the "metalled man" theme failed to survive in the medieval European version of these legends is anybody's guess (see Littleton, "Some possible Arthurian Themes," pp. 75–76.

[42] For the theory that Japan was invaded by horse-riding nomads from the Central Asian steppes, see Namio Egami, "The Formation of the People and the Origin of the State of Japan," *Memoirs of the Toyo Bunko* 23 (1964), 35–70; Gari Ledyard, "Galloping along with the Horseriders: Looking for the Founders of Japan," *Journal of Japanese Studies* 1 (1975), 217–54. See also Littleton, "Some possible Arthurian Themes," pp. 69–70.

[43] Vernadsky, *Ancient Russia* (New Haven, 1943), pp. 82–84.

The Alan of Lot: A New Interpretation of the Legends of Lancelot[1]

by Linda A. Malcor

In Littleton and Thomas's initial study of the Sarmatian influence on the Arthurian tales (1978),[2] they avoided discussion of the Lancelot corpus because they accepted the widespread scholarly view that Lancelot was a heroic reflection of the Celtic god Lleu.[3] However, I believe that the parallels between Lancelot and Lleu are not as strong as these scholars claim. Instead, I suggest that Lancelot developed from the same prototype as the Ossetic hero Batraz[4] (see figure 1) and that the core of the Lancelot corpus was formed by legends carried by the Alans, ancestors of the Ossets, who settled in the Pyrénées region in the early fifth century A.D.

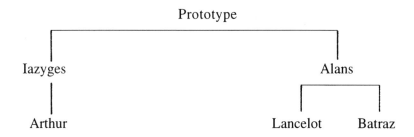

Fig. 1. Proposed Development of Arthur, Lancelot and Batraz

First, let me assess the case for the derivation of Lancelot from Lleu.[5] Both Lleu and Lancelot initially have trouble acquiring the name by which others will call them. Lancelot is often found stuck in a tree, just as Gwydon found Lleu in "Math Son of Mathonwy" in the *Mabinogion*. Lancelot originally carries an eagle, the symbol of Lleu, on his shield as his device, and both

The ideas expressed in this article are more fully developed in *From Scythia to Camelot: A Radical Reassessment of the Legends of King Arthur, the Knights of the Round Table, and the Holy Grail* by C. Scott Littleton and Linda A. Malcor (New York, 1994).

[1] An earlier version of this paper was published in *Folklore and Mythology Studies* 9 (1985), 31–49 under the name Linda A. Peterson.

[2] C. Scott Littleton and Ann C. Thomas, "The Sarmatian Connection," *Journal of American Folklore* 91 (1978), 513–527.

[3] R. S. Loomis, *Celtic Myth and Arthurian Romance* (New York, 1926).

[4] See George Dumézil, *Légendes sur les Nartes* (Paris, 1930), for the legends of Batraz.

[5] See Jeffrey Gantz, trans. and ed., *The Mabinogion* (New York, 1979), and R. A. S. Macalister, trans. and ed., *Lebor Gabála Érenn* (Dublin, 1939), for the legends of Lleu and Lugh.

heroes receive their arms and armor from a female relative associated with water. However, there are problems with this traditional argument. The legends of Lancelot contain several elements which do not parallel the mythic patterns found in the legends of Lleu. For example, Lancelot's mother is almost invisible in his legends; Lleu's mother is one of his primary antagonists. King Ban dies while Lancelot is an infant; Lleu's father is his constant companion and helper. Lancelot marries the daughter of the King of the Wasteland; Lleu marries a girl made of flowers. Lancelot's wife is loyal; Lleu is "killed" through his wife's betrayal. There are many other examples, but in short, the connection between Lancelot and Lleu is rather superficial. I am convinced that an alternate reading of the legends of Lancelot is preferable to those previously advanced.

Structural analysis of the tales of Lancelot shows that striking parallels exist not only between Lancelot and Arthur, but also between Lancelot and Batraz. Etymological and onomastic evidence reveals a marked connection between the characters in the Lancelot legends and Alan names, as well as geographic designations within areas of heavy Alanic settlement. Some of the stories appear to reflect Alan victories in battle which can be located historically in the fifth century A.D., near the time of the historic King Arthur. Through these and other examples, let us explore the possibility that the original Lancelot might have been the Alan of Lot.

STRUCTURAL ANALYSIS

In "The Sarmatian Connection" Littleton and Thomas note connections between the death scene of Batraz and Arthur's death at Kaamlan.[6] Both heroes die beside a body of water in the company of a warrior/group of warriors whom they have lead in battle. Both heroes' companion(s) refuse the task of throwing the sword into the water twice and complete the action the third time. When the sword enters the water a miracle takes place; then the body of the leader, who is dying from a head wound, disappears. Grisward[7] first noted what he calls *le motif de l'épée jetée au lac* in 1969. It was the absence of this—or any other—death scene in the Lancelot corpus which delayed the discovery of the Lancelot/Batraz connection. Indeed, it is possible that Lancelot does not have a death scene in most tales because his original death scene was the same as Arthur's and could not be used when both heroes appeared in the same story.

However, Lancelot shares several other parallels with Arthur. Guinevere is married to Arthur, but Lancelot is the one who wins the right to marry her in battle and who continues to act as her husband even after he delivers her to Arthur. Lancelot and Arthur carry twin swords which they draw from stones, and Lancelot is the only knight of the Round Table with the right to wield

---

[6] Littleton and Thomas, "The Sarmatian Connection," pp. 515–516.

[7] Joël Grisward, "Le motif de l'épée jetée au lac: la mort d'Artur et la mort Batraz," *Romania* 90 (1969), 289–340.

and Lancelot is the only knight of the Round Table with the right to wield Excalibur. There is confusion over which hero is king of Lancelot's patrimony since the continental hero defeats Claudas with troops that Arthur provides from the Round Table. Neither hero achieves the Holy Grail, and both men are tricked by a relative into begetting a son that somehow leads to their downfall.

Yet for all these parallels between Lancelot and Arthur, the greater number of parallels appears between Lancelot and Batraz: Batraz is born from a hump on his father's back beside a lake; Lancelot is first seen being carried by Ban along the shores of a lake. Batraz is associated with water and the Black Sea, and he is commonly called *du mer*; Lancelot's family restores water to the Wasteland, and Lancelot's most common appellation is *dou Lac*. Both Batraz and Lancelot avenge their father's deaths (Arthur does not). All three heroes get their swords from a kinswoman associated with water. All three heroes lead war bands. Batraz and Lancelot are not good kings (Arthur is). Batraz massacres the Narts; Lancelot kills many of his fellow knights. Batraz's body ascends into heaven; Lancelot's body ascends into heaven in the abbot's vision; Arthur's body is carried off to Avalon. Batraz does not achieve the Nartyamonga (the Ossetic counterpart of the Holy Grail) although he sees the cup; neither Lancelot nor Arthur achieve the Holy Grail, although Lancelot sees the cup. While Batraz's aunt Satana watches, he jumps into the sea shortly after his birth; Lancelot is carried into a lake shortly after his birth by either the Lady of the Lake or the Queen of the Sea. Batraz is described as the Nart "sans tache";[8] and Lancelot is traditionally "the best of all worldly knights." Given these parallels, consider the evidence for Alanic influence on the legends of Lancelot.

ETYMOLOGICAL DATA AND INTERPRETATION

The generally accepted etymology for the name Lancelot is "Lance-Lot," "Spear of Lugh."[9] However, the problem with this etymology is that *lot* in Old French does not mean light, Lleu, or Lugh. Rather, the Old French *lot* is either (1) a parcel of land or (2) the name of a river in Southern France (Aquitaine). The majority of Alanic settlements in this region have names beginning with Alan, Allan, or Allen. Occasionally the initial "A" is dropped so these syllables appear as "Lan" (e.g., "Alan d'Riano" become "Landriano").[10] Hence, Lancelot might conceivably have been "Alancelot" in the original. Gunar Freibergs has suggested that the "lanc" sequence might be a derivative of the Latin *Alanus* which was Galacized into *Alanus à Lot*, "Alan of the Lot [River]" (see figure 2). In the region of the Pyrénées it

---

8 Dumézil, *Légendes sur les Nartes,* pp. 136–137. Note that "the knight with only one flaw" in many of the legends is Bors, Lancelot's cousin.

9 See Note 2.

10 See Bernard S. Bachrach, "Another Look at the Barbarian Settlements in Southern Gaul," *Traditio* 25 (1970), 354–358.

is especially common to spell "Alanus" with a "z", e.g., Breche d'Allanz, and one of the common alternate spellings of Lancelot's name is in fact Lanzelet.[11] In southern Aquitaine the division of Lancelot's name would then become "(A)lanz-e-let" or "(A)lans-à-Lot"; and Lancelot's name in the Burgundian dialect used by Robert de Boron is in fact "Lanselot." In northern areas names there appears to be a "z" to "ç" shift, so Alenzon becomes Alençon and Lanzelet becomes Lancelot. The "à" following the "z" would have then shifted to "e" to preserve the soft quality of the "c" after the cedilla is dropped.

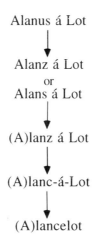

Fig. 2. Proposed Etymology of Lancelot

Note that the opening paragraph of the 1488 printing of the prose *Lancelot* is usually translated as "his surname was Lancelot, but his name at christening was Galaad."[12] What the paragraph actually says is "the people commonly [called King Ban's son] Lancelot . . . but . . . his law name [was] Galaad. And . . . he was called Lancelot *after the device of the county*."[13] According to the *Nouveau Dictionnaire Étymologique*,[14] the word *communiant* (source of the usual translation) did not come into use until 1531. But the first recorded use of *communément*, that is "commonly," is in the *Chanson de Roland*, c. 1080. Since the prose *Lancelot* as printed in 1488 did not use accents, the sound had to be replicated in another form. I submit

---

[11] Bernard S. Bachrach, *A History of the Alans in the West* (Minneapolis, 1973), p. 55.

[12] For the Paton translation, see Lucy Allen Paton, *Sir Lancelot of the Lake* (New York, 1929).

[13] This translation is my own, taken from the *Lancelot du Lac,* C. E. Pickford, ed., facsimile reproduction of the Rouen and Paris 1488 printings of the prose *Lancelot* (London, 1977).

[14] Albert Dauzat, Jean Dubois and Henri Mitterand, *Nouveau Dictionnaire Étymologique et Historique* (Paris, 1963).

that the "é" was altered to "ee" for this purpose and that the variant spelling became the source of inaccurate translation.

Another important onomastic parallel between the two traditions involves the name Ban and a variant form of Lancelot's father's name, Pant. Some forms in which this sequence appears are Uterpantdragon, Pendragon, and Benoich. The Alans originally came from the trans-Caucasian steppes and spoke a northern Iranian dialect. In Old Turkish *san* means "ten thousand" and *bon* means "strong."[15] Because of the prolonged contact between the Alans and the Altaic-speaking Huns, who eventually intruded into the Alanic territories, it is conceivable that both steppe cultures might share similar words. I suggest that *ban* is a title which is found in the original Alanic, carried to Britain by the Iazyges and to Gaul by the Alans. Hence, Alan leaders bore names such as Sangiban or Respendial, Iazyges leaders were called Zanticus and Banadaspes, and the Sarmatians and the Alans told stories of leaders called Pendragon and Ban.

Asp, which means "horse,"[16] is another Iranian element of many Alanic names, e.g., Aspar and Banadaspes. In the *Lanzelet*, Lancelot's uncle is called "Aspyol," a name with definite Iranian (and most likely Alanic) connections.

Another sequence of names involves the names of Lancelot's uncle and cousin, Boort. Boort, Boortz, Rohort, Bors, and Bort may all be variations of the Ossetic Boratä, the family of Batraz.[17] In the *Lebor Gabála Érenn*, "Alanus" is listed as the "Founder of France" when other countries were founded by figures with such original names as "Germanicus" (Founder of Germany), "Egyptus" (Founder of Egypt), and "Brutus" (Founder of Brutland or Britain).[18] Nennius records a similar legend. This origin story developed only in the Western Empire and gave the genealogy of Alanus from Noah (whose ark supposedly came to rest on a mountain in Turkey). In the Eastern Empire the origin story gave the Trojans sole credit for the founding of Europe.

The genealogies of the Grail knights—Parsifal, Galaad, and Bors—are the most extensive of all of the Arthurian heroes (see figure 3).[19] These knights are all kin of Lancelot, and the name "Alain" appears several times in their lineage. For example, Parsifal's father in the *Perlesvaus* is called "Alain le Gros de la Vales." There are many "Elaines" on both sides of the family which, for all its connection to "Helen," may be a survival of a feminine form of the name "Alain."

---

[15] George Vernadsky, "The Eurasian Nomads and their Impact on Medieval Europe," *Studi medievali* 4 (1963), 401–434.

[16] Bachrach, *A History of the Alans,* p. 98; cf. Sanskrit *ashva.*

[17] Note that Bort is also the name of a town in the region north of the county of Lot.

[18] Littleton and I discussed the Alan's connection with Ireland at length in a paper presented at the 1985 American Folklore Society National Conference in Cincinnati, Ohio.

[19] This genealogy is based on my own notes and readings of the Arthurian legends both from Britain and the Continent.

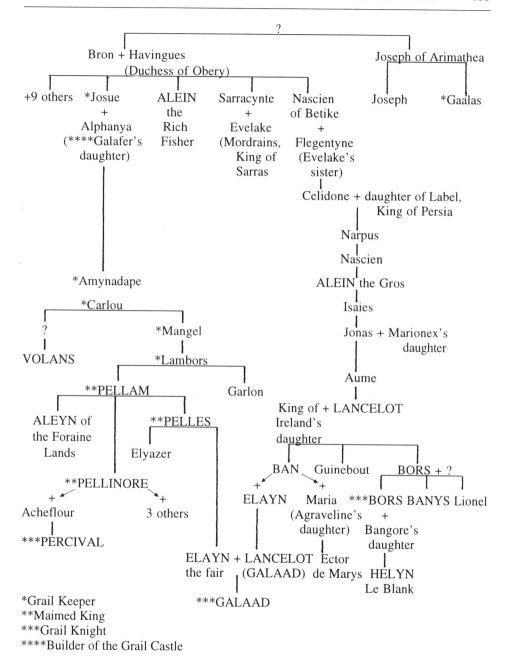

Fig. 3. The Geneologies of the Grail Knights
Derived from the Legends of Lancelot

Throughout all of these legends one element remains constant: Lancelot came from the Continent. Thus, even in the *Lancelet*, in which the action is set in Wales, many of the place and character names appear to designate French locales. For example, Dodone may sound like Dodona of Greek myth; however, note the similarity of spelling between this Germanization of a French word and the name of the French river and county Dordogne. Dodone is the dwelling place of the Lady of the Sea's antagonist, and it is in this land that Lancelot eventually establishes his household. (Incidently, Dordogne is immediately adjacent to the county of Lot.) I believe there is an historical reason for this tie between Lancelot and the locales such as Dodone-Dordogne and that this tie involves the Alanic influences upon Roman Gaul.

REFLECTIONS OF HISTORY

Honorius was Emperor of the Western Roman Empire when the Alans, Vandals and Suevii crossed the Rhine on December 31, 406.[20] Brave warriors, the Alans loved fighting and sided with whoever offered them the most in exchange for their skills. The Romans took advantage of this cultural trait and used the Alans as *laeti*—military colonists designated to control other "barbarian" tribes. In Italy, the Romans attempted to force the Alans to remain stationary. However, the Alans assimilated rapidly into Roman culture, losing their fighting ability and value as *laeti* within two generations. Therefore, in Gaul the Romans allowed the Alans to maintain their nomadic lifestyle, and these warriors, as they journeyed across the continent through the Pyrénées and into northern Spain, had a significant impact on the cultures which surrounded them.

In 414, the Alans joined with the invading Visigoths to besiege Count Paulinus of Pella.[21] The Count was a close friend of the Alan leader and at some point in the fighting the pair reached an agreement: the Alan leader would send his own wife and favorite son into the besieged city of Bazas and the Count would give the Alans land after the Visigoths were defeated. The Alans drew their wagons into a circle around Bazas and turned against the Visigoths. The Roman military commander in the region, and nominal Emperor of Western Rome, Constantius, chased the Visigoths into Spain and granted the Alans the land between the city of Toulouse and the Mediterranean Sea. Constantius asked only that the Alans control the coastal roads. The Alans accepted. (Note the parallels between this story and the earliest legends of Lancelot.) Count Paulinus of Pella's name is strongly reminiscent of the names of Grail and Fisher kings: Pellam, Pelles, Pelinore. The events themselves recall the story of Ban under siege with his wife and son endangered and the presentation of Joyous Guard to Lancelot after

---

[20] Bachrach, *A History of the Alans,* p. 52.

[21] Paulinus Pellaeus, *The Eucharisticus,* trans. Hugh G. Evelyn White (New York, 1921), pp. 331–337.

Arthur conquers Benwick on the condition that Lancelot control the coastal roads.

With the death of Valentinian III, Leo I, Emperor of Eastern Rome and his Alan general, Aspar, become the major obstacles to the "barbarian" invasions in history and to Arthur's claiming the crown of Western Rome in legend. The Alans in Gaul continued to fight for the Romans, and in A.D. 469, the Alans of southern Gaul traveled north to the region where Walter Map sets the prose *Lancelot* in order to fight a fascinating battle. Their opponent was a British king known only by his title "Riothamus" or "High King." The site of the battle is in the heart of the region which forms the geographical setting for the legends of Lancelot. In this battle, Riothamus, the man Geoffrey Ashe believes is the historical King Arthur, was wounded, last seen being carried in the direction of a town called Avalon. According to Ashe, Arthur's antagonist in this battle was the man Geoffrey of Monmouth calls "Leo, Emperor of Rome." But how could that be if Riothamus was in the Western Empire and Leo was in the Eastern Empire? Since Leo was the handpicked emperor of the Alan general, Aspar, and Riothamus was fighting Alans, Riothamus by association was fighting Leo.

This battle between Riothamus and the Alans echoes loudly in the Arthurian legends; in addition, it supplies the historical seed for the legends of the wars between Lancelot and Arthur in the final days of the Round Table. If Littleton is right, descendants of the Iazyges in Britain may well have been among Riothamus' troops. With the loss of their leader many of these troops probably never returned to Britain. After 300 years of separation, Iazyges and Alans were reunited and the legends of each group's derivative of the Batraz prototype had an opportunity to meet.

Another historical echo in the Lancelot legends involves Clovis I, the founder of the Merovingian Empire, who ruled Aquitaine and the surrounding areas c. 481–511. Either Claudas or Clovis killed Lancelot's father and stole the continental hero's patrimony from him. Claudas may well be a Romanization of the Merovingian king's name, and Clovis was the final conqueror of the Alans in Gaul during the period in which the legends of Lancelot were formed. Thus, Claudas became Lancelot's life-long antagonist and the ruler of the continent after Lancelot and the Round Table were destroyed.

ALANIC CULTURE IN THE LEGENDS

In addition to Alanic names and events in Alanic history, elements of their lifestyle appear in abundance in the legends. The Alans worshipped a god of war by thrusting a sword into the ground. The warrior who could withdraw the sword had the right to be the leader or king. Littleton has proposed that this practice served as the basis for the Sword in the Stone legend.[22] In spite of the popularity of this legend in modern retellings, no family practices this ritual more frequently in the stories of the Round Table than the knights of Lancelot's clan. For example, in Malory's *Le Mort d'Arthur*, Galaad's withdrawal of the Sword of Fate from the stone is the best-known example, but Lancelot also secures a sword from the stone altar of the chapel of Nigramorous. Also, in the *Perlesvaus*, Lancelot repeatedly draws bolts and spears from stone pillars to prove his right to pursue quests, as does Perlesvaus (Parsifal).

Another Alanic god was symbolized by a cup. The Alans are said to have worn cups as Christians through history have worn crosses. I believe this Alanic religion had a profound effect on the legends of the Grail, but I must leave that argument for another paper.[23]

Another cultural trait which seems to have influenced the legends is the Alanic practice of riding in carts. One of the first recorded legends about Lancelot tells that he rode in a cart to rescue Guinevere. Scholars have traditionally explained this scene by claiming that the ride was humiliating for a knight and that Lancelot loved Guinevere so much that he was willing to endure this shame for her sake. In the *Lanzelet*, Lancelot won the right to marry Guinevere, so technically she was his wife even though he gave her to Arthur. If Lancelot was an Alan, his wife would have been responsible for driving the cart which carried all of his worldly possessions, and if she was stolen, then the Alan would have to drive his own cart until he reclaimed her. In this light, the title commonly given to translations of Chrétien's *Le Conte de la Charrette* (literally, "The Story of the Cart"), *The Count/Knight of the Cart*, makes eminent sense.

CONCLUSION

Thus, it is my contention that Lancelot has more parallels with the Ossetic figure of Batraz than with the Celtic Lleu. I believe Arthur is a reflection of the same Alano-Sarmatian hero, but that the Arthurian legends are skewed by the presence of the historical Arthur. Given the evidence presented in this paper, as well as the additional evidence which has been amassed to date, I think we should consider the possibility that while Lancelot may incorporate some elements of the Celtic tradition, the original version of "the best of all worldly knights" might well have been an Alanic memory of a Batraz prototype as he appeared in the legends of "The Alan of Lot."

ANTIOCH UNIVERSITY

---

[22] C. Scott Littleton, "From Swords in the Earth to the Sword in the Stone . . . ," *Homage to Georges Dumézil,* ed. Edgar C. Polomé, Journal of Indo-European Studies Monograph 3 (Washington, D. C., 1982), 56–67.

[23] I have discussed this argument at length in "The Alans and the Grail, or the Theft, the Swindle and the Legend," *Folklore and Mythology Studies* 10 (1986), 27–41.